The Challenge and Urgency of Global Missions Today

E. LUTHER COPELAND

BROADMAN PRESS
Nashville, Tennessee

Unless otherwise stated, all Scripture quotations are from the Revised Standard Version of the Bible, copyrighted 1946, 1952, © 1971, 1973.

Scripture quotations marked KJV are from the King James Version of the Bible.

Scripture quotations marked NEB are from *The New English Bible.* Copyright © The Delegates of the Oxford University Press and the Syndics of the Cambridge University Press, 1961, 1970. Reprinted by permission.

Scripture quotations marked GNB are from the *Good News Bible,* the Bible in Today's English Version. Old Testament: Copyright © American Bible Society 1976; New Testament: Copyright © American Bible Society 1966, 1971, 1976. Used by permission.

Library of Congress Cataloging in Publication Data

Copeland, E. Luther, 1916-
  World mission and world survival.

  Includes index.
  1. Missions. 2. Missions, American.
3. Southern Baptist Convention—Missions. 4. United
Methodist Church (U.S.)—Missions. I. Title.
BV2061.C66 1985   266   84-14963
ISBN 0-8054-6335-6

To my students,
teachers,
and colleagues
in three institutions
in the United States
and Japan.

Contents

Preface

Preface

What is the Christian mission and how is it faring? While this book cannot promise to tell you all you want to know, it does aim to give you some of the most important information. It may even say more than you want to hear! Facts about missions, though often thrilling, are also sometimes disturbing.

In two or three ways this book differs from the usual book on Christian missions. First, it deals candidly with the question of whether American missionaries can function effectively in the non-Western world—amid the charges of neo-imperialism, crass materialism and moral bankruptcy sometimes levelled against Americans. Second, the book compares and contrasts the ways Southern Baptists and United Methodists, the two largest American Protestant denominations, have responded to the post-World War II missionary opportunity. Third, it relates the Christian mission to that issue which overshadows all others: the question of world survival in a nuclear age. Under this giant umbrella issue the book gives some attention to the relevance of the Christian mission to "the whole creation" and not merely to human beings.

Some of you may want to pick and choose where you begin reading. Therefore, in the contents I have added to each chapter title a succinct descriptive phrase or two to indicate the chapter's contents. So please select your starting place and let's be on our way. . . .

1
From a Mobile Home to a Global Mission

On May 11, 1976, I was seated on the platform of a spacious auditorium on the campus of Seinan Gakuin University in Fukuoka, Japan. This large Baptist school was celebrating its sixtieth anniversary. As chancellor, I was to deliver the Founder's Day address. I, too, was sixty years old and in my second stint as a missionary to Japan and chancellor of Seinan. For the almost twenty years between my two periods of missionary service, I had taught courses embracing the concerns of the Christian mission in relation to various cultures and religions. My travels had taken me around the globe twice. I had lived both in Japan and in India.

What a singular coincidence, I reflected, had brought Seinan Gakuin and me into being in that same year, sixty years ago, obviously quite unknown to each other! What a strange providence had drawn us together. And what a remarkable beacon had guided me from the isolation of the Appalachian mountains to an international ministry.

I thought you might want to know something of the perspective and motivation which stand behind the writing of this book. So I invite you to accompany me as I recapitulate my lifelong journey into mission.

Influences of a Mobile Childhood

The story begins early in this century in the hills of West Virginia. According to my parents, I was born in a mobile home on January 24, 1916. The nearest post office was Drennen. Now I can hear the wheels of your mind turning: *A mobile home? Way back then?* Well, it certainly wasn't the modern "mobile home" which you envision, and nobody called it that either. Our name for it was "shanty car." It was a little rectangular structure not much bigger than a boxcar which could be loaded on a log train by a cranelike, coal-fired log loader and then moved into the woods to the logging operation. Large families such as ours could put two or three of these little boxes together to accommodate their needs for housing. You see, my father worked on a log train for one of the big lumber companies which cut and milled the timber of the virgin Appalachian forests.

Before I was old enough to remember, we had moved twice. By the time I reached adulthood we had moved three more times, only once living again in shanty cars. All these moves were within the same county but almost all involved new neighborhoods, new schools, new adjustments, and the making of new friends. The fact that we were "public works" people moving into farming communities accentuated problems of adjustment.

My family continued this mobility. Of the seven children out of nine who survived to adulthood, not one remained permanently in the county of my birth and upbringing, and only one remained in our native state. Perhaps this somewhat rootless life-style prepared me for venturing into other cultures as a missionary.

But there were other important influences. These were despite the provincialism of what most would no doubt view as a backwoods environment. I rarely encountered a foreigner, and the nearest we came to other religions were two or three Roman Catholic families in the neighborhood. Yet the education of the one-room schools, grades one through eight, and the Nicholas County High School was a sound, broadening experience. And the fervent evangelical faith of Northern (now American) Baptists and Methodists helped to bring the world into view. My parents were Christians, members of Baptist churches in the various communities where they lived. The preachers and Sunday School teachers who influenced me, as well as my public school teachers, were mostly persons of some learning.

My family respected education. My mother had qualified as a public school teacher and had taught a year or two in her youth. My father, a semiorphan, had little opportunity for formal education, but he was quite bright and read widely. My sisters all became school teachers.

My oldest sister, Bertha, thought for a while that she should become a foreign missionary. Though she never followed through on this impulse, she never forgot it. Nor did I, though I can't remember having seen a missionary in my youth. Bertha was prepared to give enthusiastic support to me when I finally became a mission volunteer as indeed were the other members of my family.

Discipleship Beginnings and the Call to Preach

When I was only five years of age, I confessed my faith in Jesus Christ as Lord and Savior during a revival meeting in the little quarter-time Baptist church in the community of Enon where we were then living. The setting was quite biblical. Enon was on Peter's Creek "near to Salem" and "there was much water there" (John 3:23, KJV) —or at least enough for baptizing. At the end of the series of meetings, when the pastor asked for those to come forward who wanted to "unite with the church," I did not respond because I was not sure what his words meant.

Later, when I was eleven and living in the community of Hookersville, I was baptized in the Muddlety Creek and joined the Beulah Baptist Church. This little church was one of the "twin churches," the other being a Methodist Episcopal Church whose white frame building, almost identical to that of our church, stood nearby. Although there were the usual saws about one congregation singing "Will There Be Any Stars in My Crown?" while the other sang "No, Not One," actually we had good mutual relations. We attended each other's once-a-month preaching services and participated in each other's revivals.

Since I consider my faith experience as a five-year-old authentic, I can hardly remember a time when I did not think of myself as a Christian. The same is true for my awareness of the "call to preach" as we termed it. Among my earliest recollections are "sermons" I preached to my brothers and sisters in our backyard at the little rented farmhouse at Enon. During adolescence, however, I convinced myself that the call to preach was but a childish dream to be put aside.

When I finished high school at the age of seventeen, the country was in the throes of the Great Depression, and I saw no prospect of entering college. I worked for a while building railroads for a lumber company but I lost my job when the company shut down for two or three years. I picked and sold berries, dug and sold ginseng and other roots in the summer, and hunted and trapped in the winter to help my family make ends meet. I found great enjoyment in a vigorous outdoors life and in the solitude of the West Virginia hills.

Slowly, economic recovery began and my father bought equipment and started a small logging operation. My older brother and I joined him and we became "L. L. Copeland and Sons, Logging Contractors." We were saddled with a huge debt for our equipment.

The economic life-style of my family was that of mutual sharing: "from each according to ability and to each according to need"—and from all frugality! No doubt this pattern helped orient me to the missionary financial system in which all worked as a team, and all received the same income—not a salary but a "living stipend" as one of our missionary executives used to say. Missionaries nowadays get some increases for length of service, but in the old days one got more income than colleagues only by having more children—a system of negative finance, I assure you! Although in my career I have worked under other financial arrangements, I have been most comfortable under the system of missionary remuneration.

Now my awareness of the call to preach never had actually disappeared. When I was twenty-one it came flooding back with unmistakable intensity. The occasion was a serious accident: I fell asleep at the wheel and wrecked a log truck. The truck, which was empty, ended up on its top with the cab mashed flat. My younger brother, who was in the cab with me, was able to get out, but I was caught beneath the wreckage and could not extricate myself. The gasoline tank which was under the seat had emptied its contents upon me, and an electrical short circuit in the windshield wiper was emitting smoke! Fortunately, I was soon rescued, and the truck did not catch fire. Neither my brother nor I was more than scratched, to the amazement of any who saw the wreckage.

In the mysterious working of providence, a revival began that weekend in our little country church. Really, the accident had not seriously frightened me. I was used to living rather dangerously. But it sobered me and caused me to reflect upon the purpose of my life. *I could very easily have died,* I reminded myself, *but I had survived. Why? What was my life for?* Before the week of special services was over, I was convinced that I was called to preach, though I shared this conviction with nobody.

Then ensued a period of confusion and frustration. I knew that anyone who entered the ministry should get the requisite education. But my family was deeply in debt and I shared the responsibility for this burden. How could I pull away and go to college and seminary? Moreover, I was plagued by a sense of my unworthiness. I had a good reputation as a Christian young man, but I knew my inner weaknesses.

Meanwhile, we moved from Hookersville to Mount Nebo in the Wilderness District of Nicholas County, adjacent to what was called "the Promised Land." In that vicinity there was no active Baptist church but there were some strong Methodist congregations. The Holiness movement had invaded the area some time previously and a large barnlike Holiness Tabernacle had been erected close to our new home. I worshiped with the good folks of the Methodist churches and made warm friendships with various Christians, both of Holiness and non-Holiness affiliations. From that time, while holding strong Baptist convictions I have cherished a firm commitment to the universal church of Christ which transcends all denominational and other divisions.

It was in the Hickory Grove Methodist Church that I first confessed publicly my call to the ministry. The occasion was a revival meeting. After work, I walked several miles to attend an evening meeting. All day long I had felt impressed to give a word of testimony or exhortation that night, should there be an opportunity. Surely enough, early in the service the pastor asked for testimonies; and after two or three others had spoken, I gave my brief message. The pastor, seeing that the congregation was profoundly moved, set aside his own prepared sermon and gave the invitation at once. Several people responded, some professing faith in Christ for the first time, others rededicating their lives. Among the latter was my older brother.

Buoyed by that high tide of spiritual experience, I once again addressed the congregation, sharing with them my conviction of a call to the ministry. I remember that I said, among other things, "Here is a piece of clay placed in the Potter's hands." Our gracious Lord had shown me that just as I was, unworthy and unprepared, he could use me as his spokesman. Thus he gave me faith and courage to make my commitment. Shortly thereafter, that Methodist congregation invited me to preach my first sermon.

Pilgrimage of Preparation and Missionary Call

This public declaration of my intention to enter the ministry was in the late fall of 1939. By the next autumn I was enrolling in Mars Hill College in western North Carolina, then a junior college, at the age of twenty-four. Thus began a nine-year pilgrimage of preparation for the ministry that led to Furman University, The Southern Baptist Theological Seminary, and Yale University. Along the way my life was immeasurably enriched by the encounters with different environments as well as by the influence of some splendid Christian teachers and students.

Mars Hill, though located in an Appalachian mountain culture similar to that of my upbringing, introduced me to the Southern Baptist ethos. Furman University and Greenville, South Carolina, acquainted me more directly with the culture of the South. Louisville, Kentucky, home of Southern Baptist Seminary, is on the edge of the South and offered a much more pluralistic environment with many Roman Catholics and several Jews. Yale University was strongly ecumenical, and the New England culture was almost like a foreign country to me.

In all these various situations I found that I could communicate the gospel. With a fellow student, I helped begin a mountain mission near Mars Hill which eventually grew into a Baptist church and still exists. I was student pastor of an interdenominational community church at Linville Falls on the Blue Ridge and of American (Northern) Baptist congregations in Indiana and Connecticut.

It was in the course of this pilgrimage that my life was given more specific direction by the call to become a missionary. The crucial event in the development of this new awareness occurred at Ridgecrest in the summer of 1943. I was attending a Baptist student conference. One of the speakers was Dr. Maxfield Garrott, a missionary who had been interned in Japan at the outbreak of the Second World War and then repatriated. I little knew that after a few years Dr. Garrott would become my cherished and respected colleague in Japan.

In the midst of that terrible war, he was obviously torn between his love for his own country, the United States, and his love for his adopted country, Japan. With great feeling and firm courage, Garrott spoke of the responsibility of American Christians to love the Japanese people. "Jesus told us to love our neighbor," said Dr. Garrott. "And who is our neighbor? Japan! So we are to love the Japanese." And he continued, "Jesus also said that we must love our enemy. And who is our enemy? Japan! Therefore we must love the Japanese."

From that moment I began to feel that God was calling me to go to Japan. Why? To express to the Japanese that great, indiscriminate love of God by which he embraces all persons as his dear children,

Americans, Japanese, Russians, whites, blacks, males, females—all of us. And to express the love of Christians who have learned the meaning of God's love at the cross of Christ and now know ourselves as members of God's universal family. Of course, it was not at all clear in 1943 whether American missionaries would be able to enter Japan after the war, even if America were to win the victory. But I set my face in that direction, and it turned out that there would be a marvelous open door in Japan after the war ended. God had been preparing many young American Christians to go to Japan as missionaries just as he had prepared me.

One of these I helped to call! It was the custom of the Crescent Hill Baptist Church, located close to the campus of Southern Baptist Seminary, to have a reception each fall to welcome the students entering the seminary and the Woman's Missionary Union Training School (later called the Carver School of Missions and Social Work and merged with Southern), which was located on a campus adjacent to the Seminary. In the autumn of 1944 after I had been attending Southern Seminary for one year, a friend and I, Judson Lennon of North Carolina, although we were not new students decided that we would attend the reception at Crescent Hill Church. Upon arriving, we discovered a long receiving line beginning with the most prominent personages of the church and the two schools and ending with the lesser lights. One of us had the brilliant idea that we should fall in—unnoticed—at the end of the long line, from which vantage point we could neet the new arrivals at the training school.

Before long, Harriett Orr came by with her new roommate. I had known Harriett at Mars Hill College, and since she had already been at the Training School for a year we had renewed our friendship. Noting my inappropriate presence in the receiving line, Harriett exclaimed, "Luther Copeland, what are you doing in this line?" Being an honest fellow, I confessed to her the truth. Whereupon I introduced her to Judson and she in turn introduced Louise Tadlock from Oklahoma to Judson and me. We then dropped out of the line and accompanied the two of them. Less than two years later, Judson and Harriett were married and so were Louise and I. The Lennons are now veteran missionaries to Thailand. Louise was already a missionary volunteer, and I persuaded her that her place of service was Japan. Looking back now, I am sure that if it had been impossible for us to go to Japan we would have gone somewhere else as foreign missionaries.

So when I went to Yale University for doctoral studies in the fall of 1946, Louise went with me as my bride. My major professor was Dr. Kenneth Scott Latourette, renowned historian of missions and Oriental culture and prominent Baptist and ecumenical churchman. He had been a missionary to China in his youth but had returned to the States because of health problems. He was a warm, evangelical Christian and a wise missionary statesman. The influence of "Uncle Ken" upon me was crucial.

Exciting Adventure into Japanese Culture

Toward the end of my graduate studies, on January 8, 1948, Louise and I were appointed missionaries to Japan by the Foreign Mission Board of the Southern Baptist Convention. We could have just about as easily sought appointment with the American Baptist Foreign Mission Society except that our denominational friendships were overwhelmingly Southern Baptist. I still consider myself both a Southern and an American Baptist.

After a year of intensive Japanese language study at the Yale Institute of Far Eastern Languages, we sailed for Japan in July of 1949. By that time we had two daughters. Two more were to be born in Japan and a son was to be added after we returned to the States.

A delightful voyage of two weeks on the *President Wilson* brought us to Yokohama. We were now "real live missionaries" on Japanese soil. I must confess, however, that this journey into missionary service did not elevate me to some special sainthood. I was still a very imperfect human being, still only a sinner being saved by grace.

I have been convinced all along that the basic calling is simply to be a Christian, a loyal disciple of Jesus Christ. My calls to be a minister and a missionary were but further directions to that one basic vocation which I share with all of you. Though some of us are sent to special places and to perform special ministries, all of us are called to share Christ's mission of love and liberation wherever we are. And the special callings of some of us do not qualify us for pedestal positions above the rest. There can be no more glorious responsibility or higher position than to be a disciple of Jesus Christ.

I must admit that when we went to Japan, I had apprehensions about how the Japanese would receive us. It was relatively soon after the war, and I had known the animosities and hatreds of Americans for Japanese. Would the Japanese feel likewise toward us and our children? I did not share these anxieties with Louise because I did not want to add to whatever apprehensions she might have.

We stayed only three days in Tokyo, then went on to Fukuoka where we had been invited to live and work on the campus of Seinan Gakuin, the larger of the two schools which had been founded by Southern Baptist missionaries. It was late July, very hot and muggy, and the military train—under the Allied Occupational Government—took twenty-seven hours for the journey. It was a coal train and there were many tunnels. Since there was no air conditioning, windows had to be open. We arrived extremely tired, dirty, and a bit bewildered in the unfamiliar environment. Miss Alma Graves took us into her home, a big prewar missionary house, for two or three days until our little aluminum prefab house could be readied.

After welcome baths and a good night's sleep, Louise and I went for a walk in Miss Graves's yard and the surrounding campus. Out of somewhere to meet us came a fine-looking Japanese gentleman, immaculate in a crisp linen suit. (I never could understand how the Japanese, so poverty-stricken in those days, could look so neat and

The author, chancellor of Seinan Gakuin University, Fukuoka, Japan, 1952-55, 1976-80.

presentable!) He had a friendly smile on his face, and he extended his hand to me in the American style of greeting, saying, *"Yoku irasshaimashita! Yoku irasshaimashita!"* meaning "Welcome! Welcome!" Somehow in that simple handshake my anxieties dissipated! A Christian brother was reaching out to a Christian brother and sister across the chasm of war and bitterness, and a warm flood of Christian love engulfed us. In that moment I knew more clearly than ever before the deep meaning and the bright hope of the universal Christian fellowship.

His name was Sadamoto Kawano, and he was to be my colleague in the theological department of Seinan Gakuin University, a department which doubled as the "Seminary" of the Japan Baptist Convention. Mr. Kawano was to become one of our dearest friends, and we still have the closest ties with his family though both he and Mrs. Kawano have been dead for several years.

Then began a more intensive and delightful adventure into Japanese culture. The language, the customs, the psychology of the Japanese are so very strange to Americans. Yet we share a common humanity, and I discovered very much of the culture that is admirable and impressive. More than once, I was reminded that the universal God of truth and goodness who created us all in his image had been in Japan long before any American or any missionary arrived. He had not only sent but beckoned us to Japan. We go nowhere in the universe where he has not already preceded us and left his footprints.

The frustrations of the missionary are many, but I remember best the rewards. I recall, for example, my first sermon in Japanese. After careful preparation with the help of my private language tutor, I committed my sermon to memory. Feeling exceedingly tense and insecure, I delivered it to a little congregation on the straw mat floor of a Japanese home. What if I were to forget a crucial Japanese term? The vocabulary I was using was beyond me, and I certainly didn't know synonyms to call upon! In the midst of my nervousness, however, I observed the faces of my listeners. They were being moved! The gospel was being communicated! The Holy Spirit was giving his blessing through a very imperfect medium. I shall never forget.

Or, I was sitting in a committee session. All the others in the meeting were Japanese and of course the language was Japanese. The session was long and tedious. Then something suddenly dawned upon me: I had forgotten for the moment that I was not Japanese! I was simply one of them, and they had accepted me as such.

Seinan Gakuin and My Personal Destiny

As I have already indicated, Seinan Gakuin was founded in 1916, the year of my own birth. This has always seemed of special significance to me since my own destiny was to become so closely linked to that of Seinan. The school had been reorganized according to the educational reform measures of the occupational government. Similar to other "mission schools," it consisted of departments all the way from nursery school to four-year college, with the exception of elementary school. Enrollment was about 3000. Though closely related to the Japan Baptist Convention, Seinan Gakuin was a "legal person" and had its own board of directors as prescribed by Japanese law. In those days, aid from the Foreign Mission Board of the Southern Baptist Convention was substantial and crucial.

Two or three missionaries were already on the staff of Seinan Gakuin including Dr. Maxfield Garrott. Dr. Garrott had been elected chancellor of the school and president of the university department in 1948. He helped steer the school through the difficult process of reorganization and rebuilding.

I was welcomed as a full professor in the theological department and began teaching almost immediately. My courses were in the field of history of Christianity, but with other "Seminary" teachers I shared in the teaching of the required Christianity courses in the university as well. In the beginning I employed a seminary student as interpreter, but within a few months I began teaching—and preaching —in Japanese.

In addition to my school responsibilities, I traveled widely helping to plant and strengthen churches. I was also asked to be an associate pastor of the Seinan Gakuin Baptist Church which met on the campus. At the request of Pastor Shuichi Ozaki, I initiated an English vesper service primarily designed for Japanese who wanted to improve their use of English. This program, begun in 1949, still continues. I shared with one or two other associate pastors, all with other full-time jobs, the preaching and pastoral work of the church during a long pastorless period, 1950-1955.

In those early postwar years, Christianity was relatively popular in Japan. This was partly because the Japanese were temporarily disillusioned with their major religions, Buddhism and Shinto. Especially was the latter in trouble because the Shinto mythology had supported the imperialistic ambitions of Japan and the divinity of the emperor. In addition, Christianity shared the popularity of all things American. Missionaries and Japanese pastors had to be careful lest they welcome to the baptismal waters persons with quite superficial motivation. This phase waned by the mid-fifties.

In March, 1952, Max Garrott resigned as chancellor of Seinan Gakuin and president of the university in order to return to the States on furlough. To my profound surprise, the university faculty nominated me and the Japanese board of directors elected me to succeed him as president to take office April 1. The following autumn I was elected chancellor, whereupon I resigned as president of the university department. Sadamoto Kawano was chosen as vice-chancellor to serve with me and another Japanese professor, Shigetake Sakamoto, was elected president of the university.

At that time the school was in a severe administrative crisis, the resolution of which required some drastic and difficult administrative actions. Having seen the school through this very difficult period, I resigned as chancellor in October, 1955. As I had anticipated, Vice-Chancellor Kawano was chosen to succeed me. I was delighted that once more the chief administrative officer of the school was Japanese as had been the case for much of Seinan's history.

Not long after we arrived in Japan we had begun to suspect that our second child, Joy, who was only a few months old, had some physical problems. Eventually, her difficulty was diagnosed as cerebral palsy, probably the result of a birth injury. Her left limbs were partially paralyzed, especially the arm. Medical treatment in Japan for cerebral palsy including the manufacture of braces was not as advanced in those days as in the United States. During an early furlough, 1953-54, Joy was under the care of an American specialist who assured us that we would not need to interrupt our missionary careers on her behalf provided we could return periodically for her treatment in the States.

Nevertheless, we went back to Japan in the summer of 1954 with misgivings. Meantime, I was invited to consider a position in the teaching of missions at Southeastern Baptist Theological Seminary in Wake Forest, North Carolina. During furlough, I had taught as a visiting professor of missions and comparative religion at Southern

Baptist Seminary in Louisville. I felt that by virtue of academic training and missionary experience I was prepared to teach missions. Furthermore, I had a conviction that those who taught in this area should have had the experience of the missionary call, the appointment process, and the adjustment to a foreign culture.

International Ministry at Southeastern Seminary

For about a year, Louise and I wrestled with the question of our future. Finally, after much prayer, we decided that I should accept the offer at Southeastern. We gave a year's notice to our colleagues in Japan so there might be an orderly transfer of our responsibilities. It was in this context that I submitted my resignation as chancellor of Seinan Gakuin as previously noted.

I felt that it was important to my sense of vocation for me to be able to decide to go to Southeastern Seminary on the basis of an inner conviction and not merely because of the external circumstance of our daughter's physical condition. I relied heavily on the opinion of the specialist that we would not need to end our missionary service because of Joy's needs. However, after we had made our decision, it soon became obvious to us that Joy was suffering psychological problems because of the excessive curiosity provoked by a foreign child with a limp and wearing arm and leg braces. We now were convinced that we needed to get her back to the States for her mental as well as her physical health. With considerable trauma, we said our good-byes and left Japan.

In June, 1956, we arrived in Wake Forest, North Carolina, where I was to begin teaching at Southeastern in September. We had assumed that we could get adequate treatment for Joy at Duke University Hospital in Durham, about twenty-two miles from Wake Forest. As quickly as possible we arranged for her to be examined by a specialist in the treatment of cerebral palsy at Duke. Indeed, "God moves in a mysterious way." From the doctor we learned for the first time that there was a state hospital in Durham close to Duke Hospital, especially for children with Joy's type of impairment. The specialist conferring with us, Dr. Lenox Baker, was director of that hospital!

Consequently, Joy was admitted to this children's hospital where she received various kinds of therapy and took her second year of elementary school. At the end of the year she had operations which practically restored her leg to normal use. Very little could be done for her left arm and hand. She was on the way to a quite normal life. Today, Joy is a beautiful young woman, a professional social worker with a graduate degree in her specialty. She is happily married and is the mother of a son.

I remained at Southeastern Seminary for almost twenty years. It was my privilege to teach hundreds of students. I tried to communicate the meaning of the missionary dimension of the Christian faith, both to those who would go as missionaries and to those who would participate in Christ's mission in other ways. It is a source of great satisfaction and deep gratitude to remember that on any Sunday morning former students of mine are proclaiming the gospel and leading God's people in worship in many countries.

I sought by precept and example to encourage the exercise of critical intelligence, compassion, and sensitivity within the context of a steadfast commitment to Christ and the gospel of the kingdom of God. Along the way, I developed the conviction that our churches and their leaders must take serious account of the urbanization and secularization which is so characteristic of our age. Along with some colleagues, notably Professor Thomas A. Bland, I led in some pioneering studies in urban ministry. I tried to improve my professional competency by sabbatical leaves. The academic year of 1963-64 I spent with my family at Banaras Hindu University in Banaras, India. I profited greatly from the experience of India's ancient and rich culture and from studies in the vast laboratory in comparative religion which India affords. In 1969-70 I studied at the University of Chicago, auditing courses in missions, comparative religion, and urban studies taught by outstanding scholars.

I have published two or three books and a fairly steady flow of articles on missions and comparative religion and related studies, though my literary output is by no means voluminous. Both in writing and in public address I have tried primarily to interpret the meaning of the Christian mission to laypersons.

Through the years I have had the privilege of travel to many countries and of dialogue—both official and unofficial—with convinced adherents of the major world religions. Similarly, I have maintained ecumenical contacts within a broad spectrum of Christian diversity. I have been greatly enriched by these opportunities for mutual witness and friendship.

Back Home in Japan and Back to Raleigh

Finally, after my early experience as a missionary in Japan had long receded into the background, I received a call to return to Seinan Gakuin. In 1973, Max Garrott had become chancellor of Seinan Gakuin for the second time. In the summer of 1974 he died in the Baptist Hospital in Winston-Salem, North Carolina, after open-heart surgery. In early December, I received an Air Express letter from Seinan Gakuin. I assumed that it had to do with the twenty-fifth anniversary celebration of the founding of the university department. Being exceedingly busy, I set the letter aside and forgot about it until the next day. When I remembered and opened it, I discovered that it was from Mr. Shigetake Sakamoto, chairman of the board of directors. By now I was rather unpracticed in reading Japanese, and I laboriously made out Mr. Sakamoto's characteristically terse composition. He was notifying me that I had been elected chancellor of Seinan Gakuin and asking me to come as soon as possible to assume the responsibility!

I was completely flabbergasted! The school had not contacted me at all about this matter, directly or indirectly. However, there was a certain timeliness about the invitation. Louise and I had been thinking about going overseas again to round out our careers—or at least mine, since I am a few years older than she. However, we intended to wait until our youngest child, Luke, had finished high school. We had not seriously considered Japan because we thought it would be too difficult to go back where we had been, to get back into the language, and to enter once more into the stream of a dynamically changed and changing society. We were more inclined to go to India where we could use English!

Our decision took several months, but I'll spare you the details. The most serious problem was our concern for Luke. He insisted that we should go, but that we should leave him in Raleigh to finish high school with his friends and in his familiar surroundings. Even if he were to go with us, he could not stay at home. He would have to attend an English language boarding school in Kobe or Tokyo. Next to our decision to leave Japan many years ago, this was our most excruciatingly difficult decision.

Suffice it to say that we were reappointed as missionaries in August, 1975, and I returned to Fukuoka in late January, 1976, to succeed Max Garrott for the second time as chancellor of Seinan Gakuin.

Louise came a few months later, having stayed to see Luke through his junior year of high school and to get him well-situated for his senior year.

I had a profound sense of God's leadership in my return to Japan. It was a very emotional experience. As I expressed it at the time, "It's as though you have been away from home for some time and then receive a message saying 'Come home. We need you.' Of course, you go." Echoing in my mind were the two words the Japanese always call out in the little entrance hall of their homes when they return after an absence—whether of an hour or a year: "Tada ima!" meaning, freely translated, "I'm back!"

I was deeply gratified to discover that after the lapse of nearly twenty years, I knew almost all the directors of the school. Likewise, of the fifteen or so heads of departments all except one were acquaintances, either as former colleagues or former students. Four of them I had baptized, including the president of the University. I had left home in North Carolina to return home to Fukuoka.

Externally, at least, the Japan of 1976 was quite different from the Japan I had left in 1956. Brief visits in 1964 and 1970 had helped to prepare me for this change. The tortuous journey by train from Tokyo to Fukuoka, a distance of about 700 miles, had now been reduced to seven hours—in spite of many station stops—on the superdeluxe "New Trunk Line" trains which Americans call the "Bullet" train. On every hand were the signs of a remarkably affluent economy and a highly developed technology. Whereas I had been embarrassed in the old days because I was considered wealthy, and especially because my missionary salary was far above that of Japanese colleagues, now the situation was reversed! And in this regard I found the new conditions much more comfortable than the old.

Seinan Gakuin had changed as well. It had grown and developed remarkably. As before, it was a diversified and comprehensive educational institution with departments beginning with nursery school and kindergarten and terminating in university. Now, however, it was a large school with an enrollment of about 10,000 students. Moreover, master's and doctor's degrees were offered in two or three divisions of the graduate school. It was a true university, fully accredited, highly respected in educational circles and serving a large area of southwestern Japan and beyond. It still retained its relationship to the Japan Baptist Convention and still maintained a vital Christian witness. It had begun an international exchange program which was receiving considerable attention in Japan. It was self-supporting except for continuing subsidies from the Foreign Mission Board for the theological department, popularly known as the "Seminary." By now, those subsidies have been discontinued also. Such is the spirit of independence of Japanese Baptists.

I viewed Seinan as a mature institution, no longer dependent upon foreigners but welcoming missionaries for their contribution to its Christian witness and its international flavor. The payment by the Foreign Mission Board of salaries of the eight or ten missionaries who teach at Seinan is much more of a spiritual and symbolic contribution than a financial one, as I see it—in relation to an operating budget of twenty-five or thirty million dollars. In its maturity, therefore, the school did not hesitate to reach across the world to procure a chancellor. And it did not matter that much whether he was Japanese or American. While I was chancellor this second time, the school reimbursed the Foreign Mission Board for my salary.

My second stint as chancellor of Seinan Gakuin, 1976-1980, constituted a very busy and in many ways a very difficult period of my life. Yet it was a deeply satisfying experience. I felt that, with the help of competent colleagues, I was able to lead the school once more through some complicated problems and to strengthen in some measure its Christian character. I also served once more as one of the associate pastors of the Seinan Gakuin Baptist Church. Incidentally, during most of this time, also, the church was without a full-time pastor. It was very difficult to leave at the end of fifty months and to refuse reelection as chancellor. But we returned for furlough and for official retirement at the end of furlough in 1981.

We maintain our home in Raleigh, North Carolina, and I do quite a bit of speaking and writing in the cause of missions while pursuing a hobby or two as well. I am senior professor of missions at Southern Baptist Theological Seminary at Louisville, Kentucky, and I put in an occasional appearance there for some teaching. Louise and I have helped begin a ministry by our church, First Baptist of Raleigh, to Japanese in this area. Included is an adult Bible class which I teach in Japanese.

It has been a pleasure to have you along on my trek from a mobile home to a global mission. I invite you to continue with me as I try to describe the urgent missionary task in today's world.

2
A Universal Faith and Billions Yet to Hear

About twenty-five years ago I was participating with a team of missionaries and church leaders in an "Intelligent Faith Week" on some Florida university campuses. One member of our team was a Methodist minister from the Tonga Islands in the South Pacific. A pastor of several years experience, he was in the United States for advanced study at a Methodist seminary. Being something of a comedian, he liked to say to his audiences, "I have real Methodist blood in my veins. You see, my grandfather ate a Methodist missionary!" Then he would proceed to extol Tongan society in which well over 90 per cent of the population are Christians. From cannibals to Christians in three or four generations!

My Tongan friend's testimony was reminiscent of a striking book by Henry Van Dusen entitled *They Found the Church There.*[1] In this volume, published in 1945, Van Dusen recounts many stories of how men and women of the American armed forces, shot down or shipwrecked in the South Pacific, were swept to shore on islands whose names they scarcely knew. Expecting to find hostile, uncivilized cannibals, often they discovered friendly, literate Christians.

There was the much-publicized story, for example, of seven American airmen who were washed up on a remote Solomon Islands atoll. They were rescued, restored to health, protected from the enemy for about three months and then conducted to safety under cover of night. In the process all seven were converted to Christian faith by the islanders.[2]

A Missionary Success Story

If "they found the Church" in unexpected places during World War Two, in the succeeding four decades we have discovered all the more that the Church is worldwide. The *World Christian Ency-*

clopedia was published in 1982, a massive volume, the product of years of extensive and invaluable research. It documents the fact that the Christian Church is "for the first time in history ecumenical in the literal meaning of the word: its boundaries are co-extensive with the *oikumene,* the whole inhabited earth."[3]

Please get ready to encounter some important statistics as you read this chapter. Statistics do not make for the most exciting reading, but they are necessary to an understanding of the missionary task. Yet they should not be accepted at face value. You will find that before this chapter closes we will have raised some questions about the adequacy of statistical measurements of Christian success or failure.

There are now nearly three times as many Christians as there were in 1900. In 1980 there were almost twice as many Christians as adherents of Islam, the religion next in size to Christianity. The *World Christian Encyclopedia* reveals the startling fact that there are Christians and Christian congregations in all of the 223 countries of the world. Christians comprise the majority in two thirds of the world's countries.[4] Christianity has always claimed to be a universal religion. Now it is universal in fact as well as in ideal and intention.

It is also pointed out that the "outreach, impact and influence of Christianity have risen spectacularly" during this century. That is, "evangelized" populations, those having a general awareness of Christianity and the gospel though not necessarily responding in faith, have increased dramatically since 1900. Thus on the average each Christian today is "reaching and evangelizing" about two-and-one-half times as many persons as the average Christian in 1900.[5]

The major component of this success story of modern missions is the emergence of the churches or the Christianity of the Third World.[6] The "Third World" is a very problematical term, but it is difficult to discard because it is so convenient. Originally the "Third World" designated those areas not within the boundaries of the communist world and the world of "free nations." Later it came to mean the "developing nations." I shall use it in this discussion even more broadly, without any political overtones, simply to designate the vast territory of Africa, Asia, Latin America, and the Pacific Islands (Oceania).

We still tend to think of Christianity as the religion of the Western world: Europe, North America, Australia and New Zealand—and perhaps Latin America. The fact is, however, that a remarkable shift in the center of gravity of world Christianity is now occurring. The Christians of the young churches of the Third World are about to overtake those of the West in numerical strength. In 1980 Christians in the Western world comprised only slightly more than half of the world Christian population. If present growth rates continue, however, before the end of this century the churches of the Third World, products for the most part of the vast missionary movement of the past five centuries, will comprise a substantial majority of the world's Christians—about 60 percent. The significance of this new fact is not yet adequately understood.

In some parts of the Third World the growth of Christianity is quite remarkable. In the Republic of Korea, for example, church leaders cannot keep up with the numerical increase. In The People's Republic of China, there seems to have been a truly phenomenal growth of Christianity in spite of the dominance of Communist ideology. In Latin America, Pentecostal Christianity continues to grow rapidly.

It is in Africa, however, that there is the most widespread, consistent, and phenomenal growth. In 1900, Christians numbered less then ten million in Africa, about 9 percent of the population of the continent. By 1980 they had increased to over 200 million, more than 44 percent of the population! It is estimated that more than 16,000 new Christians are added in Africa per day.[7] Much of this growth is among "independent" churches led by African "prophets" or charismatic personalities. In terms of numerical strength, at least, Africa is rapidly becoming a Christian continent.

But there are other ways of demonstrating the success of modern missions. For instance, in 1900 the Bible, in whole or in part, was available in 537 of the world's 7000 languages. By 1980, through heroic efforts on the part of many, this number had increased to 1811, leaving 5200 languages yet without biblical translations. Likewise, in 1980, almost 37 million whole Bibles were sold and distributed, compared to about five million in 1900. The annual distribution of scriptural selections by the Bible societies now reaches more than 430 million people, 10 per cent of the world's population.[8]

The development of Christian broadcasting is even more striking. Although this medium did not even exist until the 1920s, by 1980 the total monthly audience of Christian radio and television programs had reached an astounding 990 million, almost 23 percent of the people of the world![9]

So there are evidences of a notable success story of Christian missions in the modern world.

And Yet . . .

But there are negative factors which make up the other side of the story. First of all, the rapid growth of Christianity in the modern world is in part contradicted by the fact that Christians represent a smaller percentage of global population than in 1900, and this percentage is decreasing slightly year by year. In 1900 Christians numbered about 558 million or 34.4 percent of the population. By 1980 they had increased phenomenally to 1.43 billion but comprised only 32.8 percent of the total population.[10]

The major reason for this decline in percentage of Christians to world population is that Christianity, while growing rapidly in the Third World, has suffered massive losses in the Western and Communist regions. The losses to Communism in the Soviet Union and Eastern Europe have been paralleled by defections to secularism and materialism in other areas of the Western world. It is estimated that in Europe and North America about 6,000 church members are lost to other religions or to non-religion daily![11]

Second, the distribution of Christians worldwide is still quite uneven. Though Christians are found in all of the 223 countries of the globe and comprise a majority in two thirds of them, they number less than 10 percent in fifty-one countries and less than 1 percent in twenty-four of these.[12] Two of these nations where Christians are a minority of less than 10 percent are the most populous countries of the world, China and India. The combined total of the populations of these two giant countries amounts to over one third of the people in the world. Yet Christians constitute only about 4 percent of the people of India;[13] and although there is no way to know how many Christians there are in China, the most optimistic estimates hardly bring them to more than 5 percent.[14]

Third, in many countries there are restrictions upon Christian freedom and especially upon evangelism. Over 60 percent of all Christians live in countries where civil liberties are curbed. Sixteen percent must endure severe governmental interference and harassment of religion. About 5 percent exist as crypto-Christians because to confess their Christian identity openly would endanger their lives.[15]

In 1980 there were twenty-five countries closed to foreign missions.

These included almost all the Communist nations and two or three Muslim countries. There were twenty-four partially closed, comprising the rest of the Communist world, most of the Muslim countries, and indeed practically all of the countries of South and Southeast Asia. There were eighteen other countries with some significant measure of restriction on missionary entry. On a map one can see that these sixty-seven nations represent all of continental Asia and most of Southeast Asia, over half of Europe, and a sizable portion of Africa. In the Western hemisphere Cuba is included.

All of this means that 1.3 billion persons on this globe are inaccessible to the foreign missionary presence, and over three billion are beyond the reach of uninhibited foreign missionary efforts.[16] Yet it should not be overlooked that thousands of missionaries are present in the eighteen countries with some restrictions and even in the twenty-four partially closed. It is even more important to remember that the Christian witness exists in all these countries. Though missionaries may not be present, national Christians are there, often existing as tiny minorities under severe handicaps.

A fourth qualifying factor to the success story of modern missions is the fact that about 13 percent of all Christians live in absolute poverty in various of the developing countries. They suffer all the disabilities which extreme poverty produces. Half of these members of the "church of the poor" are in Latin America, a third in Africa, and the rest in South and Southeast Asia. By the standards of the world they are paupers, living in "a condition of life so characterized by malnutrition, illiteracy, and disease as to be beneath any reasonable definition of human decency," as the World Bank describes absolute poverty. Yet in many cases they manifest remarkable spiritual dynamism and rapid church growth.[17]

Finally, it must be recognized that statistics are notoriously inadequate especially when measuring spiritual reality. The statistics cited in this discussion, from the *World Christian Encyclopedia,* have been arrived at by long and careful research. Yet they are by no means infallible. We all know that there are such things as "nominal" church membership and the radical secularizing of the Christian faith. It is impossible to know who really are Christians and who are not. What, then, is the true significance of statistics which claim to indicate how many Christians or how many church members there are? What does it mean, for example, to report that about 85 percent of Europeans (excluding the USSR) are Christians? Or about 90 percent of Latin Americans? Or about 88 percent of the inhabitants of the United States?[18] Yet these are the kinds of statistics upon which we have based our assessments of world Christian strength and missionary success.

These negative factors notwithstanding, we still claim that the modern missionary movement is a rather remarkable success story. Indeed, when we remember that most Western Christians have never taken international missions seriously or supported them adequately, the existence of the churches of the Third World seems little short of a miracle. At any rate, these young churches, now approaching half the numerical strength of global Christianity and—as we shall see—participating significantly in world missions, are a striking testimony to the success of modern missions.

American Missions in a World Context

So far as the sending of missionaries from one country to another is concerned, a vast missionary effort on the part of Christian churches and parachurch agencies is now transpiring. Worldwide, these international missionaries number about 250,000, not including short-term personnel. Though there are other missionary religions than Christianity, the world has never seen such an organized, global effort at propagation of a religious message and performance of ministries of love. About one fourth of these missionaries are Protestant (including Anglican) and three fourths Roman Catholic. Missionaries sent by the Orthodox Church number only about 1200.[19] The churches of the Third World, Protestant and Roman Catholic, are sending over 35,000 missionaries.[20] This figure is 14 percent of the total number of international Christian missionaries, a most significant statistic!

The vast majority of Protestant missionaries sent internationally come from the United States, about 70 percent as compared to only about 7 percent of Roman Catholic missionaries.[21]

About American missionaries, there is an interesting and significant phenomenon: while the missionaries sent by the mainline American denominations have been decreasing in numbers for several years, those sent by the conservative wing of Protestantism in the United States have been increasing. The present agencies belonging to the Division of Overseas Ministries of the National Council of Churches, including most but not all of the mission boards of the mainline churches, declined from a total of 5950 missionaries in 1952 to 2751 in 1980, a 54 percent decrease.[22]

Various reasons have been given for this retrenchment.[23] The boards of the mainline denominations have been prominent in international missions for a long time. Therefore they have to relate to relatively strong young churches with well-developed leadership, products of their missionary work. Representatives of these older boards believe that a dominant missionary presence and continued financial subsidies threaten the development of a healthy selfhood on the part of the young churches. This belief is shared by many if not most of the leaders of the young churches also. As a result, a fierce "missionary moratorium" debate erupted in the 1970s. Though the abrasiveness of this call for a moratorium on the sending of missionaries has abated, the imperative concern for independence and selfhood continues. We shall return to it later.

Moreover, most of the mainline denominations have suffered decreasing memberships and budgetary difficulties in recent years. Their financial problems have been made more severe by worldwide inflation. Significant, too, is the fact that the agencies related to the Division of Overseas Ministries of the National Council have been giving increased emphasis and budgetary commitment to international relief and development programs.[24]

In addition, it is likely that the current theological questioning and avoidance of theological absolutes in the ecumenical denominations has lessened zeal for missions, at least in their traditional expressions. The question of the appropriateness of conversion to Christianity of persons of other religions has been one of the most controversial issues of Christian theology for the past two or three decades. There seems to be a trend now, however, toward a renewal of evangelism in ecumenical circles, accompanied by a sensitivity toward the religious beliefs of other peoples.[25] To this question also we must return later.

On the other hand, among conservative evangelicals there has been an extraordinary increase in missionaries sent abroad in recent years, far more than offsetting the decrease of the ecumenical denominations just noted. Career missionaries sent from the United States by conservative evangelical missionary agencies increased from 9216 in 1953 to 32,101 in 1980, an astounding 248 percent increase![26] In fact, by 1980, ten out of eleven American Protestant career missionaries working overseas were sent by conservative evangelical boards and societies.[27]

These conservative evangelical agencies are of three prominent categories. First, there are the agencies affiliated with the Interdenominational Foreign Mission Association (IFMA), founded in 1917. These are forty-nine nondenominational missionary societies, often referred to as "faith missions." Second, there are the seventy-two agencies belonging to the Evangelical Foreign Missions Association (EFMA), organized in 1945 as an affiliate of the National Association of Evangelicals (NAE). In the EFMA many small denominational boards are included as well as interdenominational agencies. Several Pentecostal churches are represented. The third category is that of independent conservative evangelical agencies, not affiliated with the IFMA or the EFMA.[28] There are more than 450 of these unaffiliated agencies, most of which are quite small.

It is among these independent agencies that the most spectacular increase in international missionary personnel has occurred: from 2856 career missionaries in 1953 to 16,915 in 1980, a 492 percent increase, compared to a 143 percent increase for the IFMA and EFMA agencies. The three North American agencies with the largest numberof career missionaries are the Southern Baptist Foreign Mission Board, the Wycliffe Bible Translators, and the New Tribes, respectively.[29] All three are unaffiliated with interdenominational councils or associations of mission boards.

Reasons for the dramatic increase of international missionary personnel among conservative evangelicals are not easy to pinpoint. To a considerable extent, this missionary revival is but part of the larger phenomenon of evangelical resurgence in recent years. It is true that many conservative evangelical societies are relatively young, and their staffs and constituencies have not had to grapple with problems of relating to strong young churches overseas with aggressive leadership. Increasingly, however, they are facing these problems along with the older agencies. Nor in general is the theology of conservative evangelicals as open to doubts and questions as the theology of the mainline denominations. The former are arriving late at serious wrestling with the challenge of the world religions with their ancient traditions and their own renewed conviction of world mission.

It is from within territories traditionally non-Christian, however, that is, from the Christian churches of the Third World, that a new and burgeoning world missionary movement is now developing.

Table 1*

Number of Career Protestant Missionaries from the U.S.

1953-1980

Sent by

	Mainline "Ecumenical" Church Agencies[1]	Affiliated "Conservative Evangelical" Agencies[2]	Unaffiliated "Conservative Evangelical" Agencies[3]
1953	9,844	6,360	2,856
1962	9,892	10,983	6,249
1970	7,949	12,527	10,921
1980	2,813	15,186	16,915

* Adapted from Robert T. Coote, "The Uneven Growth of Conservative Evangelical Missions," *International Bulletin of Missionary Research*, 6:3 (July 1982), Table 2, p. 120.

(1) Those affiliated with the National Council of Churches of Christ in the U. S. A., Division of Overseas Ministries (NCCCUSA-DOM).

(2) Affiliated with the Evangelical Foreign Missions Association (EFMA), the Interdenominational Foreign Mission Association (IFMA), and the much smaller Fellowship of Missions (FOM) and the Associated Missions of the International Council of Christian Churches (TAM-ICCC).

(3) The largest of these many unaffiliated agencies are the Foreign Mission Board, Southern Baptist Convention, the Wycliffe Bible Translators and the New Tribes Mission.

Missionaries from the Third World

When I was serving for a second time as a missionary in Japan in the late 1970s, I was delighted to be reunited with many Japanese ministers whom I had taught in my stint of earlier service, 1949-1956. One of these former students, Nobuyoshi Togami, had become a missionary to Brazil and now was home on furlough. Initially, he and his wife were sent to Brazil by the Japan Baptist Convention to minister to the large community of Japanese in that country. They learned the Portuguese language, however, and gradually came to minister to the non-Japanese Brazilians as well. I was impressed with their effectiveness as furlough speakers—having done a lot of missionary deputation myself!—and I sensed that they had significantly identified with Brazil and its people. Here was a Japanese missionary

Rev. Nobuyoshi Togami (center) and Mrs. Kimiko Togami (left), missionaries from Japan Baptist Convention to Brazil, 1964-83, with Brazilian Baptist pastor (right).

couple, sent to Brazil about twenty years ago by the tiny Japan Baptist Convention which even now numbers only about 200 churches and about 30,000 members and is surrounded by an immense evangelistic task in its own society.

The Togamis are but one example of a thrilling and significant fact: the young churches of Latin America, Africa, Asia, and Oceania—almost entirely products of the modern missionary movement directed from the Western world—are now participating in ever-increasing measure in the world missionary task. They are not only receiving missionaries. They are sending missionaries. Of course, the churches of the Third World since their founding have been active in what we know as home missionary efforts, sharing the gospel with persons within their own culture.

Actually, several of them have been sending cross-cultural missionaries for some time as well. Since early in the nineteenth century Christians of the Pacific Islands churches were going as missionaries to other islanders, and not only to those of their own language and culture. In the first decade of this century, Korean churches began sending missionaries to other Asian countries.[30] Gradually, the missionary activity of the Third World churches has increased, and especially after World War II it has dramatically proliferated.

Until recently, however, there was practically no research on these missionary activities of the churches of the Third World, and knowledge concerning them was exceedingly vague. Therefore, the reports of initial comprehensive research, though admittedly incomplete, were electrifying: in 1972, a total of 211 sending agencies of Third World Protestant churches were identified, with an estimate of over 3400 missionaries.[31] A more complete survey of 1980 verified the existence of 368 agencies and an estimate of 13,000 missionaries.[32] A still more recent report indicates a total of 15,249 missionaries for 1982.[33] Even if one allows for considerable underestimating in the 1972 figure of 3400 missionaries, there must have been a spectacular increase in the ten-year period. All too little noticed is that there are also about 20,000 Roman Catholic missionaries from the Third World.[34] According to these estimates, more than 20 percent of Protestant missionaries and more than 10 percent of Roman Catholic missionaries derive from Third World churches.

This emergence of the Third World missions in the context of the shift of the center of gravity in world Christianity mentioned earlier certainly ushers in a new era of Christian missions. What this new development means for the churches of the Western world, especially those of the United States, we shall allude to later.

Those Yet Unreached by the Gospel

If the success story of modern missions is qualified by the various negative factors which we suggested earlier, it is also challenged by the huge dimensions of the unfinished task. It is a fact that there are nearly three billion people in the world who do not claim to be Christians. Almost one half of these three billion are said to be "unevangelized persons, unaware of Christianity, Christ, and the gospel."[35] There are many millions more, no doubt, who have only a vague awareness of the Christian gospel or who are prejudiced against a positive response to it.

A slightly different way of looking at the unfinished missionary agenda is to seek to delineate "unreached peoples." In the 1970s people who had been bypassed by Christian evangelism came into focus. These were variously referred to as "frontier peoples," "hidden peoples" and "unreached peoples." It appears that the term most acceptable now is *unreached peoples.* However, none of these designations is without its problems because they all identify people in relation to the Christian mission and not by their own or some neutral categories. *Unreached* is certainly objectionable to some persons who are not Christians,[36] because they maintain that they have already been reached by God or by whatever they conceive as ultimate truth or value.

For my part, I would rather use the terms *evangelized* and *unevangelized* peoples or people groups. Although *evangelized* and *unevangelized* also define peoples and groups in relation to the Christian mission, they do so more forthrightly and less ambiguously than do the terms *frontier, hidden,* and *unreached.* To say that a people group is unevangelized simply means that it is as yet unfamiliar with the Christian message—the evangel—the gospel. Conversely, those who are evangelized are those who are generally aware of Christianity. This understanding of the terms *evangelized* and *unevangelized* is consistent with the usage of the *World Christian Encyclopedia.* The WCE, however, also uses the term *unreached.* I would suggest that we abandon this *reached* and *unreached* terminology, but it is now so well-established, at least in conservative evangelical circles of missiology, that there is little likelihood that it will soon be discontinued.

With reservations, then, concerning the use of the term *unreached,* we must ask who are the people so designated? The *World Christian Encyclopedia* distinguishes separate peoples of the world on the basis of race, language, and culture. Thus it delineates about 9000 separate people groups in the world, of which something over 4000 are "Christian," that is, with at least 50 percent of their population church members. The "unreached" are only the 1000 or so of these groups "whose populations are each less than 20 percent evangelized."[37] The "evangelized," of course, are those who are generally aware of Christianity.

The editors of *Unreached Peoples,* a volume published annually since 1979, have worked from a much broader set of criteria, including religion, economic status, occupation, social position, etc., as well as the factors noted above.[38] Recently they have gone to a nonstatistical definition, considering a people unreached "among which there is no indigenous community of believing Christians with adequate numbers and resources to evangelize this people group without outside (cross-cultural) assistance."[39] Obviously, this kind of definition would mean far more unreached peoples than the criterion of "less than 20 percent evangelized" noted above.

Accordingly, the editors of *Unreached Peoples* estimate that "there are at least 15,000 major unreached people groups, the vast majority of which have not been identified as to where they are and how they can be reached."[40]

Each year this volume includes a "Registry of the Unreached." The 1984 Registry lists and indexes 3815 groups.[41] In the listing by countries, the United States and several other Western nations appear. Although the unreached in these Western countries are primarily ethnic and immigrant communities, there are also social and vocational categories. For example, in the listing for the United States, "Gays in San Francisco" are included, numbering 150,000, "Nurses in St. Louis," numbering 3000, etc.

There are still other ways of emphasizing the immensity of the missionary task yet remaining. Ralph Winter, founder and general director of the U.S. Center for World Mission in Pasadena, California, has repeatedly stressed that there are over 2.4 billion people yet unreached by the gospel of Christ—people who are beyond the scope of normal, near-neighbor outreach of any Christian congregation anywhere. Therefore they must be reached by cross-cultural missions— what we have usually called "foreign" missions.[42]

Even by the very inadequate measurement of statistics, therefore, the task confronting us as the missionary people of God is immense. Those yet unevangelized number in the billions.

But we need to probe more deeply than statistics. We must ask how we are doing in terms of the less tangible but much more important qualitative dimensions of the missionary task. Having made disciples, how successful are we in teaching them to observe all that our Lord has commanded us, as the Great Commission directs? What about our success in helping to produce everywhere the enduring qualities of faith, hope and love which the Apostle Paul understood as the distinctive fruits of the gospel? (1 Corinthians 13:13, for example). Suppose we measure our missionary accomplishments on the basis of how well we have identified with our Lord in the agenda of his own mission "to preach good news to the poor . . . , to proclaim release to the captives and recovering of sight to the blind, to set at liberty those who are oppressed, to proclaim the acceptable year of the Lord" (Luke 4:18-19).

Are we bold enough to interpret our mission as participating in our Lord's intention to bring "abundant life" in a world of grinding poverty, starvation and raw human misery? Dare we accept as the basis of our success or failure the criteria of the Judge himself in Jesus' story of the last judgment? These words are not at all intangible or abstract. They are delightfully and disturbingly concrete: " 'I was hungry and you gave me food, I was thirsty and you gave me drink, I was a stranger and you welcomed me, I was naked and you clothed me, I was sick and you visited me, I was in prison and you came to me.' . . . 'As you did it to one of the least of these my brethren, you did it to me' " (Matt. 25:35-40).

In a later chapter we shall discuss the Christian mission in relation to the fundamental human issues, the issues of survival: world peace, poverty and hunger, oppression and basic human rights, the care for the environment.

Suffice it to say at this point that the remaining task of the Christian mission is a large assignment. Indeed it is overwhelming! Humanly speaking, it appears impossible. We are encouraged by the faithful obedience and the considerable accomplishments of our predecessors. But the primary basis for our hope is the promise of our Lord that he walks with us on the path of missionary obedience: "Go therefore . . . and lo, I am with you always, to the close of the age" (Matt. 28:18-20).

He will not fail. Nor shall we if he is with us.

Notes

1. Henry Van Dusen, *They Found the Church There* (New York: Scribners, 1945).

2. Henry Van Dusen, *World Christianity, Yesterday, Today, Tomorrow* (New York: Abingdon-Cokesbury, 1947), p. 29.

3. David B. Barrett, ed., *World Christian Encyclopedia* (New York: Oxford University Press, 1982), p. 3.

4. Ibid. See Global Table, p. 6. There were 558 million Christians in 1900; 1.4 billion in 1980.

5. Ibid., p. 19.

6. Walbert Bühlman, a Roman Catholic author, uses the term the "Third Church" to designate what I am calling the Christianity of the Third World. As Bühlman sees it, the First Church was the Eastern or Byzantine Church which was prominent for

the first millenium of the history of Christianity. The Second Church was the Western Church, Roman Catholic and Protestant, which has dominated the second millenium soon to end. Now the Third Church has emerged, the Church of the Southern Hemisphere, which is destined for preeminence in the third millenium. The identification with the Southern Hemisphere is inexact and misleading but should not be allowed to detract from the significance of Bühlman's claim. See Walbert Bühlmann, *The Coming of the Third Church* (Maryknoll, N. Y.: Orbis Books, 1977), esp. pp. 3-5, 20; also *Occasional Bulletin of Missionary Research*, 4: No. 3 (July 1980), p. 98.

7. *World Christian Encyclopedia*, p. 7.

8. Ibid., p. 13.

9. Ibid., p. 19.

10. Ibid., p. 3.

11. Ibid., p. 7.

12. Ibid., p. 7.

13. Ibid., p. 370.

14. *World Christian Encyclopedia* estimates the number of Christians in the People's Republic of China at 1.8 million in a population of 890 million, or .2 percent of the population. p. 231. The *CCCOWE Prayer Day* flyer for May 22, 1983 (Hong Kong: Chinese Coordination Centre of World Evangelism) asks prayer for "700 plus open churches, tens of thousands of house churches, and 30-50 million Christians" in mainland China. The latter figure represents a range of about 3.4-5.6 percent of the total population.

15. *World Christian Encyclopedia*, p. 5.

16. Ibid., p. 17. Global Table 3 on p. 4 and Map on p. 867.

17. Ibid., p. 5.

18. Ibid. Global Table 23, pp. 782-785. For U. S. Statistics, see p. 711. This source has categories of "nominal" and "practicing" Christians, etc., but these seem to add little light.

19. Ibid., Global Table 31, pp. 802-805, with statistics updated by more recent figures for Third World missionaries.

20. Ibid., p. 17 indicates 32,500. This includes about 20,000 Roman Catholic Third World missionaries. The most recent figure for Protestant Third World missionaries is over 15,000.

21. *Mission Handbook: North American Protestant Ministries Overseas*, 12th Ed. (Monrovia, Calif.: MARC, 1980), p. 29.

22. Robert T. Coote, "The Uneven Growth of Conservative Evangelical Missions," *International Bulletin of Missionary Research*, 6: No. 3 (July 1982), p. 120.

23. See R. Pierce Beaver, *The Missionary Between the Times* (Garden City, New York: Doubleday and Company, 1968), pp. 70-72; and David M. Stowe, *Mission Handbook*, 12th Ed, pp. 9-10.

24. Samuel Wilson, "Current Trends in North American Protestant Ministries Overseas," *International Bulletin of Missionary Research*, 5: No. 2 (April 1981), p. 75.

25. Compare Stowe, *Mission Handbook, 12th ed.*, p. 13.

26. See chart in Coote, *International Bulletin*, p. 120.

27. Ibid., p. 118.

28. In addition, there are two smaller associations of missionary agencies: the Fellow-

ship of Missions (FOM), organized in 1969, with five member agencies sending a total of about 1300 missionaries; and The Associated Missions of the International Council of Christian Churches (TAM-ICCC), with six agencies sending about 200 missionaries. The ICCC is associated with Carl McIntire. For membership lists of the IFMA, EFMA, etc., see *Mission Handbook,* pp. 119-135.

29. *Mission Handbook,* 12th Ed., p. 55.

30. Martin L. Nelson, *The How and Why of Third World Missions* (Pasadena, Calif.: William Carey Library, 1976), p. 217.

31. James Wong et al., *Missions from the Third World* (Singapore: Church Growth Study Center, 1973). See especially Chapter 5.

32. Lawrence E. Keyes, *The Last Age of Missions, A Study of Third World Missionary Societies* (Pasadena, Calif.: William Carey Library, 1983), pp. 56-57, 61.

33. *Global Report* (of the Missions Commission of the World Evangelical Fellowship), January-February 1982. Cited in Overseas Ministries Study Center, *The Role of North Americans in the Future of the Missionary Enterprise* (Ventnor, New Jersey: OMSC, 1982), p. 119.

34. According to tabulation of statistics in the *World Christian Encyclopedia,* p. 803. Australia and New Zealand are excluded from the statistic on Oceania.

35. *World Christian Encyclopedia,* p. 19. See Global Table 30, p. 798. The criteria for determining to what degree a people is evangelized are very complex. See pp. 117-121.

36. See Stanley J. Samartha, "Partners in Community . . .," *Occasional Bulletin of Missionary Research,* 4: No. 2 (April 1980), p. 80.

37. *World Christian Encyclopedia,* p. 19. See pp. 105-115.

38. Edward R. Dayton and Samuel Wilson, eds., *Unreached Peoples '83* (Monrovia, Calif.: MARC, 1983), p. 494.

39. Ibid. Compare pp. 494 and 499.

40. Ibid., p. 493.

41. Ibid., 1984, 41 Ibid., pp. 347-710.

42. See, for example, Ralph Winter, "The Task Remaining . . .," Ralph Winter *et al., Perspectives on the World Christian Movement: A Reader* (Pasadena, Calif.: William Carey Library, 1981), pp. 312-326.

3
"An Endless Line of Splendor . . ."

We have looked briefly at where we are in the world missionary task, but how did we get where we are? Unless we understand something of our past, we cannot possibly discern our responsibility in the present. After all, the history of Christian missions is our history. You and I would not be Christians if our faith had not spread from the place of its origin in Palestine. So we need to look back at least as far as Pentecost.

How about putting ourselves to a little test? As we read this chapter, let's pause occasionally and ask ourselves where we would have stood on some issue affecting missions had we been living then. (*In the Middle Ages would I have been on the side of Francis of Assisi and Raymond Lull, denouncing the use of force in converting Muslims? Or would I have made my "bold mission thrust" with a Crusader's sword?*)

I have suggested that we look back to Pentecost. Something tremendous happened on that notable day. The disciples began their trek through history and throughout the world. A poet has called this stream of missionaries "an endless line of splendor."[1] Well it isn't all splendor but much splendor. Some splendor and some shame. The splendor is the love of Christ and love of others which inspired unstinting service. The shame is the distortion of the gospel of Christ from time to time by forcing people to become Christians, disdaining their culture or refusing them places of leadership in their own churches.

But the missionary lineage is actually far more ancient than Pentecost. The Bible reveals God as having a mission from the beginning. His mission is to redeem his creation which has been corrupted by human sin. So he called a particular people, Abraham and his heirs, to share his mission. Through them "all the families of the earth were to be blessed" (Gen. 12:2).[2] They were to be "a light to the nations" so that God's salvation might "reach to the end of the earth" (Isa. 42:6; 49:6).

The universal redemption promised in the Old Testament for "the latter days" (Isa. 2:2; Mic. 4:1) was finally accomplished in the life, sacrificial death, and triumphant resurrection of Jesus of Nazareth.

Pentecost confirms the thrilling fact that the new age of the promised salvation has now dawned. So Peter declares that the prophecy of Joel has been fulfilled (Acts 2:16-21). The Holy Spirit has been poured out "upon all flesh" and the floodgates of God's mercy have been opened universally so that "whoever calls on the name of the Lord shall be saved."

Though Pentecost has many meanings,[3] supremely it signifies that the Spirit empowers the whole church—including us—for our task of universal witness. The newly constituted people of God "were all filled with the Holy Spirit and spoke the word of God with boldness" (Acts 4:31).

Spontaneous Missionary Expansion
in a Hostile Environment (To AD 323)[4]

This worldwide understanding of the gospel was not achieved without difficulty. The book of Acts records a spread from Jerusalem in ever-expanding waves as the gospel, under the leadership of the Holy Spirit, leaps over barriers of religion and race and of the disciples' prejudices. Frank Stagg calls this movement "the early struggle for an unhindered gospel."[5] He takes his cue from the last word of the book of Acts, "unhindered," a word which in one form or another occurs several times in the book.

In the beginning the witness was confined to the Jews and prose-lytes gathered in Jerusalem for the feast of Pentecost (Acts 2:5-11), therefore still within the boundaries of Judaism.

Before long, however, Philip was preaching the gospel within a new circle, the hated Samaritans, people of mixed race and garbled religion, not Jews but not quite Gentiles. Those who believed were baptized and received the Holy Spirit just as had the Jewish believers (Acts 8:5-25).

Then Philip carried the gospel across another barrier. He preached the good news to an Ethiopian eunuch. Although this black Gentile was already a participant in Jewish belief and worship, presumably he was barred from full acceptance as a Jewish proselyte because he was a eunuch. However, there was nothing to "hinder" his baptism and full inclusion in the New Covenant people of God (Acts 8:26-40).

Another hindrance was overcome as Peter preached the gospel to the Romans of Cornelius' household. These Romans were "God-fearers" who had accepted the faith of the Jews in the one God but had not become official proselytes. Even so, it took a vision from heaven to convince Peter that he should break Jewish taboo and enter the home of these uncircumcised Gentiles and eat with them! They received the Holy Spirit and there was no "hindrance" to their baptism (Acts 10:1 to 11:18).

Driven by persecution, the disciples were thrust out beyond the more familiar circle of the Romans who occupied Palestine into the Greek (Gentile) world at large. At Antioch in Syria some of these Jewish Christians began preaching to Greeks also. So a new dimension was reached, and Antioch became the new center for a mission to the larger world, including Gentiles as well as Jews. Also, at Antioch Paul came into prominence as the greatest of the missionaries and interpreter of the universal mission.

Finally the really crucial question concerning the Christian mission had to be faced. The problem seems not to have been whether Gentiles could receive the Christian message but whether those who believed had to be circumcised and observe the Mosaic law, as an influential "Judaizing" party among the Christians demanded (Acts 15:1). In short, the question was, Do Gentiles have to become Jews (proselytes to Judaism) in order to be saved?

The result was a conference in Jerusalem described in Acts 15 and Galatians 2—or more likely two conferences whose results have been blended together in Acts 15.[6] The first agreement seems to have been that indicated in Galatians: Gentile believers did not need to be circumcised, and the Jewish believers associated with the Jerusalem church would give major attention to evangelizing the Jews while Paul and his colleagues at Antioch would give priority to the Gentile mission. When the Judaizers continued to make trouble, another conference worked out the compromise indicated in Acts 15, asking the Gentile Christians to observe certain dietary and other restrictions which would be non-offensive to their Christian brothers and sisters who were Jewish.

If I had been one of the Jewish Christians, where would I have stood?
with Paul? with James? with the Judaizers?

So the gospel, under the impetus of the Spirit of the risen Lord, had been freed from the hindrances of race, religion, and prejudice and was operating in the world of universal humanity. Actually, it was creating a *new* humanity in which the old distinctions of race, cult, social status, and sex had no crucial significance. All that mattered was the new creation in Jesus Christ (Gal. 3:28; Col. 3:11), an ideal still difficult for us Christians to attain.

Amazing Spread in Spite of Persecution

Persecution at the hands of Jewish leaders had been present from the first. But eventually the massive power of the Roman government was unleashed against the young and growing church. This persecution was sporadic but sometimes devastating.

Many stories of martyrs are preserved. One of the best attested and most dramatic is that of Polycarp, Bishop of Smyrna and disciple of the apostle John. Polycarp died at the stake at a venerable old age, in AD 155, under the reign of Antoninus Pius. Arrested by the Roman authorities, no threats could frighten the old saint or disturb his poise. When urged by the proconsul to swear by Caesar and reproach Christ in order to save his life, Polycarp replied with the famous words: "Eighty and six years have I served Him, and He never did me any injury: how then can I blaspheme my King and my Saviour?"[7]

In this early period, the blood of the martyrs was the seed of the church, and a truly remarkable expansion occurred. Faithful missionaries such as Paul and his companions were succeeded by Pantaenus, Gregory the Wonder Worker, Mesrop, and others.

Perhaps even more important than the careers of these who were in a special sense missionaries was the witness of the "nameless ones" —Christians engaged in secular callings who gave convincing witness wherever they were but whose names are unknown to us.

> Merchants . . . traveling along the Roman roads told their message in conversation, as did tradesmen in their stores, craftsmen in their workshops, and soldiers in their camps or on route march.[8]

Thus, by what appears to have been a remarkable spontaneity, the Christian faith spread all over the Roman empire. Within about three hundred years it had become a force with which the empire had to reckon. Also, it had spilled over the boundaries of the empire into Edessa, Armenia, Mesopotamia, Babylonia, Persia, parts of Arabia, and almost certainly into faraway India.

Expansion of a Christian Empire (AD 323-1792)

With the emergence of Constantine as the sole Roman emperor in 323, a vast change occurred in the situation of Christianity and the Christian mission. The empire now had an emperor who confessed to be a Christian, and the Christian religion which had been persecuted with increasing intensity soon became the official religion of the Roman empire. Especially under Constantine's successors, paganism was suppressed, pagan temples were destroyed by Christian mobs and, sad to say, Christians, the erstwhile persecuted, became the persecutors.

Christianity was corrupted by political power, and conversion became too much a matter of policy rather than conviction. Mission was perverted into the expansion of a "Christian" empire or civilization. This pattern was to continue for many centuries. Yet these unfortunate aberrations were in part counterbalanced by a succession of devoted missionaries.

Expansion amid Chaos (AD 323-800)

Already by the time of Constantine's accession, Christianity was agitated by inner conflicts over doctrine and discipline. Before these controversies had run their course, the great barbarian invasions shattered the empire and threw Roman civilization into eclipse in western Europe, ushering in the Dark Ages of European history.

Again, before recovery could come, the militant religion of Islam erupted to wrest many traditional strongholds from Christianity. Within a century (AD 632-732) the Muslim Arabs had carved out an empire which dwarfed the Roman Empire at its largest extent. Under Muslim rule, Christians were allowed to exist under certain restrictions but not to evangelize Muslims. Consequently, in the Muslim areas Christianity either died out or was reduced to small minorities turned in upon themselves.

During this period monasticism came into prominence as the characteristic missionary agency. The monasteries provided the personnel for frontier missions, and on the frontier itself they became the institutions for Christianizing and civilizing the barbarians.

An example of the missionary monks was Wynfrith, better known as Boniface (about 672-754). Boniface went from his own country, England, to the continent of Europe, where he laid the foundations for Christianity in what is now the Netherlands and Germany. He brought many of his fellow Englishmen to help in the conversion of Europe and was especially notable for the utilization of women monastics in his missionary work.

Among other things, Boniface is famous for the episode of the oak of Geismar in Hesse. With an axe Boniface attacked the great oak, sacred to the god Thor, in the presence of Thor's devotees. While the pagans waited to see Thor strike Boniface, a blast of wind finished Boniface's work and split the tree in four parts. Convinced that Boniface's God was the stronger, the pagans were converted to Christian faith, and Boniface built a church out of the timber of the oak! While still performing missionary labors in a ripe old age, Boniface was martyred by a band of marauding pagans.

Missionary monks not only carried on extensive work in Europe. Some who were followers of a bishop named Nestorius, who was labeled as a heretic, penetrated central Asia and even reached China in the seventh century, where they built churches and monasteries. This Nestorian Christianity died out in China after about two centuries, however, because of persecution and perhaps because it remained too foreign.[9]

Yet the missionary expansion was not a total monopoly of monks. Christian merchants trading beyond the borders of the empire took the gospel with them, as did Christian captives carried into other countries. For example, Axum, a region of northern Ethiopia, was converted by laypersons of both these categories.

The Conversion of Europe (AD 800-1492)

On Christmas Day, 800, an event transpired which had great significance for the history of Europe: the Pope crowned the Frankish king, Charlemagne, as Roman emperor. This act symbolized the renewal of the Roman empire in western Europe and set the stage for rivalry with the eastern empire, which still survived with Constantinople as its capital. The coronation of Charlemagne also signalled the passing of the Dark Ages.

Charlemagne set the fateful precedent for conversion at the point of the sword. He did not hesitate to use military coercion and violence to bring pagans to the baptismal waters.[10]

The Western church centering in Rome and the Eastern church centering in Constantinople gradually pulled apart, primarily because of cultural differences, politics and economic rivalry. This separation is generally considered to have become final in 1054. The frequently conflicting interests of Constantinople, Rome, and the Germanic princes caught Europe in crosscurrents of military and missionary activity.

For all the superstition and violence of the Middle Ages, there was an impressive attempt on the part of the church to Christianize Europe, to create a Christian culture, a more ambitious attempt than ever before or since. The authority of the church over European life was an amazing phenomenon, though it began to disintegrate before the period ended.

Monasticism continued as the missionary agency. The missionary monks went beyond the imperial frontiers of Europe with Christian nurture and civilizing education. The great preaching orders, the Dominicans and the Franciscans, helped to vitalize the missionary spirit and make the message more evangelical.

The amazing Francis of Assisi, founder of the Franciscans, not only went boldly to preach the gospel to the hated and feared Muslims. He also preached to the birds and animals, calling them as well as the sun, fire, and other forces of nature, his brothers and sisters. All too rare in the history of missions, he seems literally to have believed that the gospel is God's good news to "the whole creation" and not just to us human beings.

Concentration on Christianizing Europe left little time for attention for the larger world beyond. Besides, the Americas had not yet been discovered by European explorers and the Muslims stood between European Christians and the vast continent of Asia. Several times fierce invaders from Asia who had already been converted to Islam threatened Europe. In the eleventh century the Seljuk Turks overran the Middle East and made Christian pilgrimages to the Holy Land hazardous. European Christians answered with the misguided zeal of the Crusades. This tragic episode has so embittered the memory of Muslims that many seem almost immune to the Christian message. In the thirteenth century the fearsome Mongols conquered their gigantic empire, the largest the world had ever seen, protruding into a sizable section of Europe. The missionary response to them was too little and too late. Nevertheless, missionaries again penetrated India and China, and this time some were Roman Catholics as well as Nestorians. Unfortunately, once more Christianity soon died out in China. Then when the Ottoman Turks succeeded the Mongols and advanced upon Europe in the fifteenth century, they were already Muslims and European Christendom was beginning to disintegrate. The Turks captured Constantinople in 1453 and transformed the great church of Saint Sophia into a mosque.

For the most part the attitude of European Christians toward Muslims was hostility, the crusading mentality. Yet there were a few persons besides Francis of Assisi who carried the Christian message into Muslim lands at the risk of almost certain death, insisting that converts must be won not by force but by earnest preaching, careful persuasion, and fervent love. Outstanding among these was Raymond Lull (1232-1316), born on the Mediterranean island of Majorca. A playboy in his youth, Lull experienced a dramatic conversion. The result was a long life given to efforts to win Muslims by methods consistent with the gospel. In his old age, Lull was stoned to death by Muslims in North Africa. Thus he exemplified the conviction by which he had lived: "He who loves not lives not; he who lives by the Life cannot die."[11]

Where would I have been? with the Crusaders? or with Lull?

New Worlds Appear (AD 1492-1649)

With the voyages of discovery by Christopher Columbus and others whole new continents appeared before the eyes of European Christians, the newly discovered Americas and the newly accessible continent of Asia.

The Roman Catholic Church eagerly entered into this enlarged world. In 1493 the Pope drew a line through the Atlantic Ocean from the North to the South Pole, the region to the west to belong to Spain and that to the east to Portugal. Upon the monarchs of these two powerful Catholic countries was laid the obligation to Christianize their respective territories. Earlier monastic orders, especially the Franciscans, Dominicans, and Augustinians, were joined by the new Society of Jesus (Jesuits) to comprise a great missionary force. Missionaries went everywhere that the explorers and colonists penetrated and even beyond to establish frontier missions.

Thus the pattern of close alliance of missions and cultural and political expansion continued. Roman Catholic expansion was often accompanied by forced conversion in much of the New World. Fortunately, some missionaries courageously opposed this violence and cruelty. An example is Bartoleme de Las Casas (1474-1566), a Spanish priest who spent a long life championing the cause of Indian rights. The writings of this sixteenth-century Spaniard sound strangely modern.

During this period the foundations were laid for a Roman Catholic Latin America. The Philippines, also, became Roman Catholic except for the Muslim population especially numerous on the southern island of Mindanao.

Roman Catholic missionary efforts in Africa had little permanence until a later period, but the faith was planted in most of the countries of Asia, to survive with varying degrees of difficulty. The great Francis Xavier (1506-1552), a charter member of the Society of Jesus, introduced Christianity to Japan in 1549, where it flourished for a time only to be driven underground by terrible persecution in the next century. Xavier died while making plans to enter China, but a fellow Jesuit from Italy, Matteo Ricci (1552-1610), born the year Xavier died, re-introduced the Roman Catholic faith to China in 1583. Very astutely, Ricci and his Jesuit colleagues tried to relate the Christian faith to Chinese culture. However, after a controversy which lasted almost two centuries, the Papacy ruled in favor of a more rigid stance.[12]

Meanwhile another new world had appeared. Martin Luther (1483-1546) had discovered the bright new world of the Pauline understanding of the gospel: justification by grace through faith. The result was the Protestant Reformation, an event of immeasurable significance for Western history.

By this discovery of the gospel of grace, Luther and his fellow Reformers "restored the substance of missionary preaching."[13] Regrettably, however, their world missionary vision was deficient. There were practical reasons for this deficiency, such as their lack of direct contact with non-Christian lands and their rather all-consuming struggle to establish and maintain the Reformation. And of course they had abandoned the monastic system which was the great Catholic instrument for missions.

But they also had some theological views which were not supportive of missionary concern.[14] Typical were the notions that the Great Commission applied only to the apostles and had in fact been fulfilled by the apostolic preaching, that the imminent end of the world gave no time for missions to the nations and that whatever missionary responsibility there was for pagan lands rested with the Christian rulers who were laymen. Exaggerated views of God's sovereignty and election also tended to put a low premium upon human efforts and organizations for mission. In the seventeenth century these ideas developed into a rigidly anti-missionary apologetic.

There were some exceptions to these perverted views. A notable example is Justinian von Welz (1621-1668), an Austrian nobleman and layman. By his writings von Welz strongly challenged the anti-missionary polemic of the Lutheran theologians.[15] Harshly put down but determined to act upon his convictions, he went as a missionary to the Dutch colony of Surinam where he met an early death.

Of great significance were the Anabaptists who were among the first to insist that the Great Commission was binding upon all Christians.[16] Despised as heretics and subversives by Protestants and Catholics alike, the Anabaptists lacked status and opportunity and so their vision was deferred for later fulfillment.

What would have been my stance? That of the Lutheran theologians? Or von Welz?

Preparation for Change (AD 1649-1792)

Gradually the colonizing Roman Catholic powers of Europe, notably Spain and Portugal, were superceded by Protestant countries, especially the Netherlands and Great Britain. The first Protestant missions accompanied colonial expansion and were directed or subsidized by the governments or the commercial companies which managed colonial development.

Meanwhile a new understanding of mission was emerging which tended to break this tie of dependence upon the colonizing agencies. This new view was associated with Pietism, which began in Germany in 1650, and with Puritanism in Great Britain and its American colonies.

The Pietists sent missionaries to Greenland, to south India, and to the Jews in Europe. Perhaps more important than their own missionary efforts was their influence on other Protestants. It was through the influence of Pietism that a group of refugees in Germany, having fled Roman Catholic persecution in Bohemia and Moravia were organized into a unique missionary church, the Unity of Brethren, more commonly called the Moravian Church. In this zealously missionary community, all the members were committed to the task of missions. They went near and far as missionaries, and those who could not go worked to support those who went. The Moravian Church brought to new expression the ideal seen earlier in the Anabaptists, that every member of the church, ordained or unordained, is a missionary.

Puritan missionaries ministered to colonists and Indians in the American colonies. John Eliot (1604-1690), while serving as pastor in Massachusetts, did a notable missionary work among the Indians. He produced the first Bible in an Indian language which likewise has the distinction of being the first Bible printed in America in any language. Eliot's Bible was in the Algonquin or Mohican language; unfortunately the Mohicans later became almost extinct and this Bible became a museum piece. Eliot was supported by what seems to have been the first Protestant missionary society, organized in 1649 and later known popularly as "The New England Company."

David Brainerd (1718-1747) likewise had a notable missionary ministry among the Indians, though his life was cut short by tuberculosis. Brainerd's life and diary, published by Jonathan Edwards, was extremely influential on later missionaries.

The Great Century (AD 1792-1910)

1792 marks the beginning of a great new missionary thrust in Protestant missions. The prophet for this new missionary era was William Carey (1761-1834). Under Carey's inspiration and leadership the Baptist Missionary Society was organized in England in 1792. In that same year Carey published his famous *Enquiry into the Obligations of Christians to Use Means for the Conversion of the Heathens.*

A few years earlier Carey had stood to propose this same question as a theme for discussion in a Baptist ministers' meeting. Whereupon an older Baptist minister, with strict views on predestination and election, ordered him, "Young man, sit down, sit down! You're an enthusiast. When God pleases to convert the heathen, He'll do it without consulting you or me."

Carey's little book was a calm, tightly reasoned statement of missionary responsibility which effectively countered the anti-missionary arguments inherited from the Protestant Reformers. Carey also backed up his promotion of missions with his life and example. At great personal sacrifice he went to India in 1793 to begin a long and illustrious missionary career, never to return to his native land. Carey and his Baptist colleagues, by the soundness of their principles and the amazing breadth of their missionary approach, set a high standard for missionary work which followed. Thus a humble, self-educated shoemaker became known as "The Father of Modern Missions."

Within a few years after the founding of the Baptist Missionary Society, the other Protestant denominations in Europe and the United States had organized for missions, either with denominational or interdenominational boards and societies. Thus Protestants finally had missionary agencies to parallel the long-standing monastic orders of Roman Catholics.

The late Kenneth Scott Latourette, renowned historian of missions, called the nineteenth century the "great century" of missions and also the "Protestant century." Although Roman Catholic missions continued with vigor, "the expansion of Christianity took place through Protestantism even more than through Roman Catholicism,"[17] he said.

As for the Eastern Orthodox churches, many of them had long been hemmed in or submerged by Islam. However, the Russian Orthodox Church moved across the vast expanse of Siberia in the nineteenth century and even planted churches in Alaska and Japan.

During this period there was a serious attempt to engage the whole church in the work of missions. Increasingly, Christians who never went as missionaries were involved through active interest, prayers and financial support of missions. For the first time in the history of missions, women began to participate in significant numbers in the actual work of missions, both as missionary wives and as single missionaries. This involvement of women was true not only of Protestants but also of Catholics, through the latter's orders of nuns. Of special importance were women's missionary societies, which were organized both to send missionaries and to take initiative in missionary support and missionary education in local churches.

Even in this "great century" of foreign missions, however, leaders had to struggle against lethargy, indifference, or even opposition to foreign missions on the part of the majority of those who called themselves Christians.

A broad approach was generally characteristic of nineteenth-century missions. Not only preachers, but teachers and doctors were sent, along with many other specialists in literature, church development, and community services. The conviction was that the gospel must be communicated by deed as well as by word.

By and large, missionary agencies were organized independently of governments, but missions were by no means free of political entanglements. Such could hardly be expected in the heyday of Western colonialism. In a country such as India, for example, the fact that most of the missionaries were from Great Britain, the colonizing country, had inevitable complications. And even in China, which was not "colonized" in the formal sense except for small enclaves such as Hong Kong and Macao, both opium and the gospel found entrance at the point of British guns! In Africa, missionaries preceded the colonizers and often urged the extension of colonial rule, in part for their own protection. It was common for the colonial powers to subsidize the mission schools and other agencies for community development. Though many discerning missionaries tried to preserve and to transform the cultures of those among whom they worked, by and large it was assumed that Christian missions and Western civilization went hand in hand. Nor were missionaries free of the racial and cultural prejudices and superiority complexes of the West. Such attitudes bred paternalism: the nationals were often considered incapable of administering their own churches and missionary institutions, at least without a long period of tutelage. The "station" approach, fairly typical of the nineteenth century, was criticized for uprooting nationals from their own culture. That is, the tendency was for the missionaries to live in compounds containing a cluster of mission institutions which drew nationals in as converts and employees.

The ideal, articulated by such missionary statesmen as Henry Venn of the Church of England and Rufus Anderson of the American Congregational Church, was the "three selves": developing churches that were self-supporting, self-governing, and self-propagating. In too many instances, however, missionaries held on to power and leadership. And in any case the three selves described an independent church, not necessarily an indigenous church, that is, one vitally related to its environing culture. The churches, with few exceptions, remained entirely too Western. It should not be surprising therefore that many thoughtful Asians and Africans would view Christian missions as but the religious aspect of Western imperialism.[18]

For all its defects, however, the nineteenth-century missionary movement manifested great heroism. It was the age of outstanding missionary pioneers and statesmen. Their numbers are far too great even for honorable mention here. In many places missionaries suffered great hardships and met early deaths. West Africa, especially, was known as the "white man's graveyard" because of its oppressive climate and the tropical diseases to which white persons had no immunity. In the first fifty years of the work of the North German Missionary Society in Togoland, sixty-four of its 157 missionaries had died and fifty-eight had been invalided home.[19] In the first nineteen years of the Nigerian mission of Southern Baptists, twenty white missionaries were sent out. Four died in Africa and all the rest were forced to return to the States because of illness.[20] These cases are not unusual. It is said that until the middle of the nineteenth century very few missionaries to Africa survived more than two years![21]

Nor should we forget that Christian ideals had a profound influence upon the various cultures: the abolition of the slave trade, the planting of the seeds of freedom and democracy, various social reforms, and even reforms in other religions such as Hinduism were in large measure due to the influence of Christianity during the "great century" of Christian missions.

Ecumenical Cooperation in a Time of World Upheaval (AD 1910-1947)

For missions, the first half of our century was a period of "advance through storm."[22] In 1914-18 a war was fought which was so universal in its involvements and effects that it was called a "world war." In about thirty years another world war, even more universally devastating, was waged. Sandwiched in between was the great economic depression which was also worldwide. Accompanying World War II was the Holocaust, the appalling slaughter of over six million Jews by the Nazis, and the development of weapons of total destruction—nuclear bombs.

These cataclysmic events inhibited missionary expansion, but even so some very significant developments occurred within missions. Among these were the new expressions of interdenominational cooperation which we call the "ecumenical movement".

For two reasons the modern missionary movement was largely responsible for the rise of the ecumenical movement: (1) by means of modern missions Christianity became aware of itself as a worldwide fellowship, and (2) the modern missionary movement nurtured the growing conviction that the unity and mission of God's people are inseparable, according to the prayer of our Lord "that they all may be one . . . that the world may believe" (John 17:21).

This period begins with the great World Missionary Conference convened in Edinburgh, Scotland, in 1910. This assembly was preceded by many interdenominational missionary conferences on the "mission fields" and here at home and by the formation of agencies for interdenominational cooperation in missions and in the work of the churches in general. The Edinburgh Conference was the fulfillment of the vision of William Carey. This farsighted missionary statesman had proposed such a conference for 1810, but his suggestion had been dismissed as nothing more than a "pleasing dream."

The Continuation Committee of the Edinburgh Conference brought into being the International Missionary Council, whose organization was delayed until 1921 because of the turbulence of World War I and its aftermath. Another stream flowing from Edinburgh 1910 resulted in the organization of the World Council of Churches in 1948.

The series of great world missionary congresses sponsored by the International Missionary Council, beginning with Jerusalem in 1928, gave increasing accent to the developing maturity of the "young" churches which were products of modern missions. At the Whitby, Ontario, conference in 1947, about one third of the delegates were from the young churches. At Whitby, as never before, the ecumenical partnership between older and younger churches in the task of world missions was manifested and celebrated.

Thus the churches of Asia, Africa, and Latin America were manifesting their independence of control by foreigners, paralleling the movements for political independence from the colonial powers which were already underway before the end of World War II.

Missions in a New Era of
World Christianity (AD 1947 to the Present)

We have now arrived at the contemporary period in which, as we noted in the previous chapter, Christianity has become for the first time truly worldwide with the center of gravity of world Christianity rapidly shifting from the Western countries to the Third World.

This new era, like the previous one, is a period of revolutionary, breathtaking change. It has brought unprecedented challenges to Christian missions. However, we will not unduly prolong this chapter with a discussion of the contemporary period, because that is what the rest of this book is about.

Let me venture a word of evaluation of the history of missions since 1492, after nearly five hundred years of domination of the Western nations over the rest of the world. We have noted some of the defects of this missionary movement: the inevitable association of Christian missions with the colonial enterprise, the superiority attitudes of many missionaries, the tendency of missionaries to hold on to control over the young churches and their agencies, and so forth.

However, many missionaries refused superiority attitudes and practiced the ideal of equality set forth by Carey and other pioneers. Many proudly introduced the culture of their adopted land to their homeland and made lasting contributions to international relations. And what we must acknowledge as cultural arrogance on the part of many was often offset by their genuine love for those among whom they worked. I have heard Japanese Christians in moments of confidential sharing reminisce about a pioneer missionary, perhaps how he butchered the Japanese language, how he was difficult and autocratic, etc., only to end with the statement, "But he loved us, and we could forgive his mistakes." Missionaries in many places could give similar reports. Love has indeed covered a multitude of foibles, errors of judgments and just plain sins on the part of us missionaries.

Who can estimate adequately the value of what missionaries have done: introducing countless persons to eternal salvation, helping transform individuals and institutions for the better, translating the Bible into hundreds of languages, providing essential services such as education, medicine and agricultural improvement, and inspiring governments to develop systems to meet these needs . . . ?

For all the defects, there *was* much splendor in the missionary movement.

Notes

1. Vachal Lindsay, "Foreign Missions in Battle Array," *Masterpieces of Religious Verse,* edited by J. D. Morrison (New York: Harpers, 1948), p. 507.

2. Repeated in Gen. 18:18; 22:18; 26:4; and 28:14.

3. On the missionary meaning of Pentecost, see Harry R. Boer, *Pentecost and Missions* (Grand Rapids, Mich.: Eerdmans, 1961).

4. Periodization in this chapter is considerably influenced by J. H. Bavinck, *An Introduction to the Science of Missions* (Philadelphia: Presbyterian and Reformed Publishing Company, 1960), pp. 275-305.

5. Subtitle of Frank Stagg, *The Book of Acts* (Nashville: Broadman Press, 1955).

6. Compare Ferdinand Hahn, *Mission in the New Testament* (Naperville, Ill.: Allenson, 1965), pp. 77-86.

7. *The Ante-Nicene Fathers,* Vol. I (Grand Rapids, Mich.: Eerdmans, 1953), p. 41.

8. Basil Mathews, *Forward through the Ages* (New York: Friendship Press, 1951), p. 11.

9. See K. S. Latourette, *A History of the Expansion of Christianity,* Vol. II (New York: Harpers, 1938), p. 279; and Laurence E. Browne, *The Eclipse of Christianity in Asia* (Cambridge: Cambridge University Press, 1933), pp. 99-101.

10. Latourette, ibid., p. 105.

11. Mathews, ibid., p. 74.

12. For a brief discussion of this "Rites Controversy" see K. S. Latourette, *A History of Christian Missions in China* (New York: Macmillan, 1929), Chapter VIII.

13. Gustav Warneck, *Outline of a History of Protestant Missions* (New York: Fleming H. Revell, 1902), p. 11.

14. Ibid., pp. 11 ff.

15. Ibid., pp. 32 ff.

16. Franklin H. Littell, *The Anabaptist View of the Church,* second edition (Boston: Starr King Press, 1958), Chapter IV.

17. K. S. Latourette, *A History of the Expansion of Christianity,* Vol. IV (New York: Harpers, 1941), p. 33.

18. See, e. g., K. M. Panikkar, *Asia and Western Dominance* (London: George Allen and Unwin, 1959), pp. 279 ff.

19. John Aberly, *An Outline of Missions* (Philadelphia: Muhlenberg Press, 1945), p. 224.

20. H. C. Goerner, *Exploring Africa* (Nashville: Broadman Press, 1950), p. 90.

21. Ralph Winter, in *Perspectives on the World Christian Movement: A Reader,* ed. Ralph Winter *et al.* (Pasadena, Calif.: William Carey Library, 1981), p. 169.

22. Title of vol. VII of K. S. Latourette, *A History of the Expansion of Christianity* (New York: Harper, 1945).

4
This Crucial Day: "The First Cry of a Newborn World"

The period since World War II is an era of breathtaking change, the era of "future shock." Tomorrow rushes to meet us before we have adjusted to yesterday. If one understands revolution to mean "a sudden, radical or complete change" or "a basic reorientation and reorganization,"[1] then this postwar period has witnessed several world revolutions occurring simultaneously. Three of these seem to be particularly significant especially with regard to Christian missions: the breakup of the Western colonial empires, unprecedented advances in technology, and the missionary revival of world religions.

The Liquidation of Western Colonial Empires

Our generation has witnessed the end of almost five centuries of Western dominance of the world through colonial empires.

If one looks at a prewar map of Asia and Oceania, say in the 1930s, he will perceive that almost all of that vast area was under the control, directly or indirectly, of Western powers. Russia had already moved across the broad expanse of Siberia, and the British empire stretched through South and Southeast Asia embracing more than a subcontinent. The East Indies were under the control of the Netherlands and the Philippines under the United States. The French had their Indochinese empire. Oceania was parceled out among the various Western powers. China, the most populous nation in the world, while not colonized formally except for the tiny enclaves of Macao and Hong Kong was actually at the mercy of the Western powers and Japan. Only Japan and Thailand had escaped foreign control, and Japan was well on the way to her own empire building with the Western empires as her model.

In the 1930s Africa was even more completely a checkerboard of European empires. In North Africa, Libya, Egypt, and Ethiopia had for the moment some semblance of independence. But in the rest of Africa only Liberia was in the hands of Africans, and in this little nation the ruling elite were not native Africans but descendants of freed slaves from the United States.

In the Americas the situation was much more complex. For the most part, the large empires based in Europe had long since been broken up—British, French, Spanish, Portuguese. But it was the descendants of Europeans who dominated in most of the Americas, and not the aboriginal populations or the imported blacks. The United States was vulnerable to the charge of "internal colonization" because of the treatment of native Americans and blacks. Moreover, in the Caribbean area, American and European control remained strong.

Now in the past forty years or so a sweeping revolution has occurred by which Western colonialism in the political sense has been almost entirely liquidated.

The Birth of New Nations

In Asia, the independence movement was already well-advanced before World War II. As a result, India became an independent nation in 1947, at the price of partition whereby Pakistan became a separate country for Muslims later to become the two nations of Pakistan and Bangladesh. The independence of Burma, Sri Lanka (Ceylon), Malaysia, and Singapore soon followed, all parts of the former British empire. Meanwhile, the United States had granted promised independence to the Philippines in 1946.

The Japanese conquests of East and Southeast Asia had liberated several areas from the controls of the European powers. Accordingly, when the latter, after the defeat of the Japanese in 1945, attempted to reinstate their colonial rule, they met with armed resistance. As a result, nations such as Indonesia, Vietnam, Kampuchea, and Laos emerged. In Asia and Oceania, about thirty new nations have been born out of the disintegration of the colonial empires.

Practically all of Africa has been freed from colonial control. The liquidation of the British African empire began with the independence of Ghana, the former Gold Coast, in 1957. The dismantling of the other colonial empires followed. In Africa and its offshore islands more than forty new nations have emerged. An ambiguous situation remains in South Africa: Namibia is a colony of the Union of South Africa, which is controlled by a white minority of European ancestry.

In the Caribbean, the breakup of colonialism has been much less complete. About a dozen entities in this area remain under American, British, French, or Dutch control.

There are still Western colonial possessions remaining here and there in other parts of the world: Macao and Hong Kong on the edge of China, and a few island territories in the Indian Ocean, off the coast of Africa, and in the Atlantic including the lately disputed Falklands or Malvinas. These vestiges notwithstanding, the era of nearly five centuries of Western colonial empires has ended.

Colonialism under New Guises

But there are other forms of colonialism, somewhat more subtle, which are very much alive in the "postcolonial" world. Minorities in many places are sometimes victims of an "internal colonization," that is, treated as inferiors and exploited. The Soviet Union has vassal states in Europe whose autonomy is violated, and she has subjugated and absorbed the peoples of Central Asia, the most recent example being Afghanistan.

In many cases, a Western ideology captures the loyalty of a minority in a given country, who then by whatever means gain power and control the majority. Marxism is especially adept at this kind of exploitation. But there are also right-wing, Fascist ideologies which have seized control in many situations, especially in Latin America. In a number of cases many of the former victims of political mastery by Western nations are now controlled by a Western ideology. This invasion by a minority ideology, whether of the left or the right, is a kind of colonialism—or more exactly, imperialism—whereby people are subjugated and controlled often with the most brutal violation of basic human rights.

Then there is the matter of economic imperialism. The developed nations, especially the superpowers by means of multinational corporations, are able to control world markets, to evoke consumer demands, and to produce wealthy minorities in the developing countries while making more severe the poverty of the masses.

So people of the developing nations of the Third World, most of which have a history of control by Western powers in the colonial era, now see themselves as victimized by a new imperialism stemming from the West. Their perceptions of Western colonialism in a new guise, to which we must give some attention in a chapter six, cannot fail to have a harmful effect upon Christian missions, especially those operating from a Western base.

From Hiroshima to Silicon Valley: the Technological Revolution

A second dramatic development of our times is the technological revolution, actually a cluster of different revolutions but with technology as their prime source and sustainer. The result is a massive and many-sided revolution which not only *in toto* but in any one of its prominent aspects may be as important as the industrial revolution of two centuries ago.

Under a Mushroom Cloud

Consider, for example, the discovery of atomic fission by which the "nuclear age" has been initiated—with such ominous threat as well as bright promise.

On July 16, 1945, in preparation for the use of this newly developed weapon on selected cities of Japan, the first atomic bomb was exploded in the New Mexico desert. The thunderous boom of sound was described as "the first cry of a new-born world."[2] The scientist who had directed the project and had watched the "unbelievable light" from a bunker eleven miles away remembered the "very solemn mood" of the watchers. "We knew the world would not be the same," he recalled. "A few people laughed, a few people cried. Most were silent."[3]

More than a year later after the events of Hiroshima and Nagasaki, Pierre Teilhard de Chardin, brilliant philosopher-scientist, reflected upon that explosion in the Western desert as follows:

> The thing had happened. For the first time on earth an atomic fire had burned for the space of a second, industriously kindled by the science of Man.
>
> Man, stunned by his success, looked inward and sought by the glare of the lightning his own hand had loosed to understand its effect upon himself. His body was safe; but what had happened to his soul?[4]

Since 1945 we human beings have known that we grasp within our hands awesome power sufficient to extinguish the human race and most other life upon this planet. And not only the shadow of the mushroom cloud of annihilation by nuclear bombs is terrifying— whether in the hands of the superpowers or lesser powers who know

Hiroshima, 1945. Destruction from atom bomb blast.

the secret and have produced the weapons. Even the peaceful use of nuclear energy is desperately feared by many because of inadequate safety precautions and the threat of pollution by nuclear waste.

For about thirty-five years I have had intimate contact with a nation of people who know themselves as the only victims, thus far, of atomic bombs, and who know my country as the only nation, thus far, to have used these awesome weapons. I have stood silent, humble, deeply moved, in the presence of artifacts of the atomic bombings in the Peace Museums of Hiroshima and Nagasaki. I have viewed the charred remains of the uniforms of school children who were victims. I have seen the stark, lifelike reproductions in plastic of grotesquely distorted limbs and faces of some who survived—at least for a time.

Indeed, history was changed in the summer of 1945. Do we yet really know what happened to us then?

Sputniks and Interplanetary Space

On July 20, 1969, with millions of eyes fixed upon him by means of their television sets, one of us earth dwellers for the first time set foot upon the ancient desertlike surface of the moon. As he took his first, almost weightless step, Astronaut Neil Armstrong exclaimed, "That's a small step for a man, a giant leap for mankind!"

This "giant leap" for humankind was indeed but one small, faltering step into space, preceded by many other steps and to be followed by how many others we do not yet know. In the background were several decades of the development of rocketry by which space travel was made possible. Then followed a long series of launchings of satellites and space probes, without and then with human passengers.

Today, artificial satellites are commonplace, and probes of the planets, as yet without astronauts, are adding richly to the store of human knowledge of the universe.

Under the sponsorship of the National Aeronautics and Space Administration (NASA) and otherwise, impressive plans for the "colonization of space" have been drawn up. In the artificial habitat of a space colony, we are told, thousands of people can live, perform various occupations, including intensive agriculture, and raise their families.[5]

The "space age," less than three decades old, is a revolution in human affairs far more impressive, I should think, than the discovery of the "new world" by Columbus in 1492. What does it portend? Will we export our earthly conflicts and violence to the extraterrestrial universe? Our astronauts had hardly returned from the moon when we were told that American military space strategists had "conceptually devised a plan for the installation of interspace ballistics missiles on a moon base."[6] Having polluted much of the good earth and destroyed many of its species of living creatures, will we now pollute and rape the planets and the stars?

Or will our ventures into space give us a new perspective upon our own planet, a new sense of our oneness with each other and our environment? Are the words of Jerry Brown, former governor of California, prophetic of our future? "As we spend more of our time in space," said Governor Brown, "we'll spend less of our time thinking about racial, linguistic and cultural differences. . . . That's a lot better than war. We'll gain an Earth view instead of a nationalistic view."[7]

Somewhere in that vast expanse of mystery will we encounter creatures of a superior intelligence, as many believe, fulfilling the mythological projections of our science fiction? Or will we finally have to conclude that we human creatures, with our ambivalent potential for such heroic good and such horrendous evil, are God's best hope for the responsible stewardship and priestly care of his good creation?

The Information Society

> Had the automobile developed at a pace equivalent to that of the computer during the past 20 years, today a Rolls Royce would cost less than $3, get three million miles to the gallon, deliver enough power to drive the Queen Elizabeth II, and six of them would fit on the head of a pin![8]

So awesome has been the meteoric rise of computers that a journalist was impelled to such a ludicrous exaggeration!

Ours is the age of telecommunications, that is, devices which substitute the electron for paper as the medium of communication.[9] By the early years of this century telephones were commonplace, having largely replaced the telegraph. In the 1920s radio became an important medium of mass communication; and in the 1950s television came into its own, ready to utilize the communications satellites to be provided later by the space age.

With the passing of two more decades, computers had added their transforming presence to the picture. So the systems of mass communication were augmented by systems for the mass storing and retrieval of knowledge and the multiplication and manipulation of information.

Already the communications revolution is well under way, but the new systems are destined to further transform the way we live in ways we can hardly imagine as they move into our homes, offices, factories, and all our institutions. It is expected that before long home computers will become as omnipresent as televisions. The "media room" is already appearing in homes, a room for large-screen televisions and stereophonic systems with storage space for video cassettes, audio tapes, phonograph records, and the computer unless there is a separate computer room.[10] Our methods of learning, manufacturing, banking, commerce, travel, entertainment—all aspects of modern life —are being radically changed by the communications revolution.

It has been suggested that our grandchildren, exposed to the new means of acquiring and assimilating knowledge, may be the first "genius generation."[11] Thus some see the future of the information society in utopian visions, the development of a unified, global civilization with a democracy of information and the evolution of a higher and more ethical intelligence.[12]

Others warn of "the decay of purposive information,"[13] the increase of trivia, the deterioration of literature[14] and the distortion of communication, both intentional and unintentional.[15] At worst there are portents of an Orwellian nightmare with the control of information by unscrupulous persons in places of power. Especially threatening is the secret storage of information about individuals. At best, this is an invasion of privacy. At worst it is a means to exploit and damage persons.

Therefore, as with other aspects of the contemporary technological revolution, the "brave new world" of the information society is also clouded by the ambiguities and unpredictability of human nature.

All This and More—in a Secularizing Milieu

The nuclear age, the space age, the information civilization—these are but some of the most prominent aspects of the technological revolution of our day. One could add others. For example, there is the development of the "pill" which almost overnight significantly altered the sexual mores of the United States and other countries where people can afford such easy means of contraception. There are the dramatic developments in medical science and in genetic engineering. Or there is the phenomenon of urbanization, the mushrooming of metropolises and megalopolises by which the world, only yesterday predominantly rural, is fast fulfilling the predictions of an urban world before the end of this century.

It is this multifaceted technological revolution which has brought the future racing toward us with such hurricane-like velocity.

Undergirding the revolution, while at the same time nurtured by it, is the secularizing process which is so pronounced in modern life. Secularization may be defined as the process by which human beings relate to the world as that which they are to comprehend and control, allowing no religious views or authorities to impede this comprehension and mastery.

Where secularization advances, religion comes under serious challenge, though the modes of religious reaction may vary.[16] The characteristic effects are the erosion of religious beliefs, the displacement of religion from the center of life, and the emergence of secular substitutes for traditional religions.

A concomitant of secularization is "secularism." Often secularism is no more than a vague, blurry assumption that all that is or all that matters is found within this world, that is, within the natural order and the realm of human achievement.

However, it is difficult if not impossible for human beings to live in the kind of neutral relativism which secularism implies. If we deny a transcendent or "religious" ultimate, we are apt to substitute a secular one. So we construct our gods out of the secular stuff of life, and a secular faith or quasi-religion results: materialism, the worship of money and the things which money can provide; scientism, our worship of our science and technology; hypernationalism, the exaltation of our nation-state as that demanding ultimate commitment; racism, the inordinate evaluation of our race to the denigration and subjugation of others, etc.

Often such secular faiths are unorganized and unrecognized, even unconscious. In some cases, however, they develop structures which parallel the usual cultic structures of religion: authoritative documents (scriptures), creeds and dogmas, rites of initiation and dedication, charismatic leaders, etc.

Communism, for example, is a secular ideology with the characteristics of a religious cult. It has its own dogmas concerning the nonexistence of God, the sole reality of the material world, and the inevitability of the class struggle. At the present stage of its development, its authorities differ from place to place, whether Lenin, Stalin, Ho Chi Minh, Mao Tse Tung, or the post-Maoist leaders of China, and so forth; for it is by no means monolithic. It nurtures a strong eschatological hope for a utopian society, and it requires of its devotees firm commitment and faithful service to hasten the coming of the new day. It has been noted that the party's organization resembles that of a church and its membership a kind of "lay priesthood of experts."[17]

As represented by regimes in many nations, Communism at best denies some basic human freedoms. At worst, it is ruthless in its repression. But so too are right-wing Fascist regimes which are also expressions of secular idolatries.

Some other varieties of secular faith are not such obvious replacements of religious commitment. Materialism, for example, may be the actual religion of some of us who profess the Christian faith. Or some overarching quasi-religion such as the "American way of life" may subtly overlap and supercede traditional faith.

Religions in a Changing World

Traditional faiths also are changing. In the mid-1960s I attended a conference of American and Indian scholars in New Delhi. In a time of free discussion, an elderly Indian gentleman arose to ask rhetorically, "Why is it that so many Americans are suffering from nervous and mental disorders?" Then he proceeded to answer his own question as follows: "We Indian people know how to have inner peace because of karma and samsara. We need to share the spiritual riches of India with our American brothers and sisters."

Of course, this statement may be criticized as overly naive. If the ancient notions of karma, the principle of cause and effect, and samsara, reincarnation or transmigration of souls, have helped people to be content with their life situations in India, they have also served to condone gross inequities and injustices. And it can be documented that psychological illnesses increase with the growth of technological urbanism. India, too, will have this problem as it urbanizes.

But my point in recalling this incident is that it illustrates a common phenomenon: a conviction on the part of Hindus and adherents of other religions that their traditions have a message for the world and that they need not be intimidated by the universal spread of Christianity. Such an attitude is common today, and we need to realize that it represents a very significant change.

Reviving Religions

At the beginning of this century, and even until the end of World War II, it was generally assumed by missionaries and other Westerners that the great non-Christian religions would soon die out. They were too weak, backward, and superstitious to ward off the onslaughts of science and secularism, it was thought. This assumption has proved to be premature. Most of the world religions, though corroded by secularism, have experienced revival. So our age of massive secularization, however contradictory it may seem, is also an era of resurgent religious activity.

One major source of this revival of world religions is cultural renewal. The nations emerging from colonial domination take new pride in their own traditions, and religion is newly emphasized as inseparable to traditional culture. In addition, there is a rediscovery of the inner meanings of the religion involved. Interestingly, in the case of Hinduism, and to a lesser extent other religions, researches by Western scholars of religion helped to disclose a spiritual heritage in part forgotten or overlooked by people under colonial subjugation. Also, there has been an attempt, sometimes quite deliberate, to counteract the Christian mission, the latter being viewed as the religious wing of Western imperialism. So the domestic religions have girded up their loins to resist the foreign invader.

In any case, in today's world the religions often exhibit a new sense of confidence. They feel that although Christianity and other forces from the West have been confronting them for a long time, they have withstood the confrontation and can now face Christianity without a sense of inferiority. With some of them, revival and the new sense of confidence have inspired a contemporary missionary effort.

The Current Religious Scene

The current religious scene is more variegated and complex than ever before. There are the traditional "living religions" which are studied in the typical course in the history of religions or comparative religion. These are the religions originating in Western Asia, Zoroastrianism, Judaism, Christianity, Islam, and the newer arrival, Baha'i;

the religions born in India, Hinduism, Jainism, Buddhism, Sikhism; and the religions deriving from Eastern Asia, Taoism and Confucianism of China, and Shinto of Japan. In addition, there are the religious systems associated with tribal or preliterate societies still existing in various places in Asia, Australia, Oceania, Africa, and the Americas. These are often called "primal religions." Examples are the religions of the native Americans.

To add further variety, in many parts of the world there has been a mushrooming of new religions, usually called "cults"—though I doubt if anyone wants his religion to be called a "cult." Many of these new religions are derivatives of one of the traditional religions, but they are often syncretistic, blending together elements from various religions.

Next to Christianity, Islam is the largest and most aggressively missionary of the older religions. It is the dominant religion in many countries, particularly in northern Africa, the Middle East and parts of Asia. Worldwide Islam claims about 800 million adherents.[18] There are about 2 million Muslims in the United States,[19] most of whom are affiliated with the American Muslim Mission, formerly the Nation of Islam (Black Muslims) but now representing orthodox Islam and seeking to reach out beyond the black community. (The Nation of Islam also continues as a minority movement.)

Baha'i grew out of the Islamic context in Iran over a century ago but is now a world religion in its own right. It is zealously missionary, hoping to lead all people to accept the teachings of its prophet, Baha-'u'llah (1817-1892), and become united in one world faith, thus overcoming divisions and ushering in world peace. The 1980 world membership of Baha'i was estimated at 3.8 million, of whom about 210,000 were in the United States.[20]

Zoroastrianism, or Parseeism, the ancient religion of Persia (Iran), was once an influential faith. It left its imprint upon Judaism and thus indirectly upon Christianity. Now, however, it is reduced to a tiny minority of about 150,000 adherents,[21] mostly in Iran and India, and apparently has no sense of missionary responsibility.

Adherents of Judaism exist today in the state of Israel and as minority populations in many countries, especially in North America where they have found a haven from persecution—except for occasional outbreaks of anti-Semitism. There are about seventeen million Jews worldwide.[22] Judaism impresses the world not least by its sheer existence in spite of everything, especially after the horrible Nazi Holocaust in which over six million Jews were murdered.

Since the early centuries of the Christian era, Judaism has not usually been overtly missionary. Recently, however, some Reform Jewish leaders in America have encouraged missionary activity, especially directed toward the "unchurched," as a matter of survival.[23] There is concern that American Judaism may die out because of defections to other faiths, losses by intermarriage, and lower birth rates.

Hinduism is the ancient religion of India, having developed through the centuries into a very diverse and complex religious system. Traditionally, Hinduism was not concerned with expansion beyond the boundaries of Indian culture. Generally Hindus espouse religous tolerance and the mutual acceptance of the various religions as valid, not conversion from one to another. In modern times some missionary activity has accompanied a reaction to Christian missions and a new sense of pride in things Indian.

Religious movements related to Hinduism in the United States include Vedanta societies, found in many American cities; the International Society for Krishna Consciousness, popularly known as the Hare Krishna movement; the Divine Light Mission led by Guru Maharaj Ji; and the World Plan Executive Council which sponsors the Transcendental Meditation (TM) programs. There are about 500,000 Hindus in the United States.[24]

Buddhism, though an ancient derivative of Hinduism, has been missionary from its beginning. It spread mostly eastward to become the great religion of Southeast and East Asia. The world population of Buddhism is about 275 million.[25]

Buddhism is represented in the United States by several organizations. There are the Buddhist Churches of America, deriving from a Chinese and Japanese type of Buddhism, which report something near 100,000 members.[26] Nichiren Shoshu (formerly known as Soka Gakkai) is a Japanese variety of Buddhism which carries on aggressive missionary work in several countries. About 235,000 members are reported in the United States.[27] Zen Buddhism has few official adherents in the United States, but its influence is rather pervasive.

The ancient Chinese religions, Taoism and Confucianism, have never been missionary in any active sense, but both have spread wherever the influence of Chinese culture has extended, especially in Southeast Asia, Mongolia, Korea and Japan.

The onslaught of communism has been devastating to Chinese religions. It appears that Confucianism and Taoism now have their greatest strength in Taiwan and Hong Kong and in the Chinese immigrant communities in many parts of the world.[28]

The native religion of Japan is called Shinto, meaning "way of the gods," to distinguish it from the religious "ways" or systems which entered Japan from China in early times. Shinto is essentially a primal religion, with belief in many gods, which has managed to continue into the modern period and survive in a sophisticated society.

Shinto is not missionary, but some of the new religions in Japan, many of which are related to Shinto, are seeking to spread worldwide. These "new religions" have emerged in Japan in the last hundred years or so, many after World War II. Several have followings in the United States. Among these are Tenrikyo ("Heavenly Reason Teaching"), The Church of World Messianity, Seicho-no Ie ("House of Growth"), and PL Kyodan ("Church of Perfect Liberty").[29] All four of these are seeking, with varying success, to reach beyond the borders of the Japanese immigrant community to Americans in general. The Church of Perfect Liberty is said to have been the most successful so far in reaching American blacks and Hispanics—as well as whites.[30] It claims over 50,000 families in the United States.[31]

East, West, and the Future

So the Eastern religions, by missionary efforts and by various other cross-cultural means, are making their impact upon the Western world. What does this portend for the future?

In a notable essay published in 1947, the late historian of cultures Arnold J. Toynbee made a striking set of prophecies. He predicted that historians a century later, in AD 2047, would note that what was most significant about the twentieth century was the impact of Western civilization upon the world. After another millenium, 3047, historians would be impressed by the effect of Eastern religions and ideologies upon the West. By 4047, a unitary world culture would have emerged. And, suggested Toynbee, the historians of 5047 would say that the importance of this unification of world cultures "was not to be found in the field of technics and economics, and not in the field of war and politics, but in the field of religion."[32]

Since Toynbee made these projections in 1947, the impact of the revolutionary developments of Western technology upon the East has intensified. But so also have the influences of the Eastern religions and cultures upon the West. I suspect that Toynbee's timetable could be moved up a few hundred years—maybe a millennium or two!

In my judgment, the remarkable revolutions which we have noticed do indeed portend that if the world survives long enough, we are headed toward a blending of East and West in a unitary world history and world culture though that does not mean uniform or homogeneous. Nor does it mean the end of conflicts, though one hopes that these can be contained to prevent universal disaster.

I make so bold as to predict—or to confess my faith—that out of it all Jesus Christ shall emerge as the center of world history, as he has been the center of the ambiguous and violent history of the West which has often denied him and contradicted his spirit but has been unable to displace him.

For me, this is one element in the faith which undergirds the Christian mission.

Notes

1. One of the definitions in *Webster's Third New International Dictionary* (Springfield: G. & C. Merriam Company, 1971), p. 1944.

2. William L. Lawrence, cited in Jim Garrison, *The Plutonium Culture* (New York: Continuum, 1981), p. 21.

3. Julius Robert Oppenheimer, cited in ibid., p. 21.

4. Pierre Teilhard de Chardin, *The Future of Man* (New York: Harper and Row, 1964), p. 140.

5. Richard D. Johnson, ed., *Space Settlements: a Design Study* (Washington, DC: NASA, 1977); and T. A. Heppenheimer, *Colonies in Space* (Harrisburg, Pennsylvania: Stackpole Books, 1977).

6. James C. Sparks, *Moon Landing: Project Apollo* (New York: Dodd, Mead and Company, 1969), p. 102.

7. Quoted in Margaret Poynter and Arthur L. Lane, *Voyager* (New York: Athenuum, 1981), p. xiii.

8. A writer for the *Washington Star*, quoted in Edward Cornish, ed., *Communicating Tomorrow: the Coming of the Information Society* (Bethesda, Maryland: World Future Society, 1982), p. 45.

9. Joseph P. Martino, "Telecommunications in the Year 2000," in Cornish, ed., *Communications Tomorrow*, p. 30.

10. Cornish, ed., *Communications Tomorrow*, p. 5.

11. Alan P. Hall, in Cornish, ed., *Communications Tomorrow*, p. 11.

12. See, for instance, Yoneji Masuda, "The Information Civilization: the Challenging Upward Trail for Humanity," Howard F. Didsbury, ed., *Communications and the Future: Prospects, Promises and Problems* (Bethesda, Maryland: World Future Society, 1982), pp. 69-73. However, Masuda admits some serious problems.

13. Essay by that title by Gerald M. Phillips, in Didsbury, ibid., pp. 337 *ff.*

14. See Michael H. Begnal, "The Future of Literature," in Didsbury, ibid., pp. 3-6.

15. See Michael Marien, "Non-Communication and the Future," in Didsbury, ibid., pp. 62-68.

16. For an interesting and insightful discussion of the different modes of secularization in the European continent, in England and in the United States, see Martin E. Marty, *The Modern Schism* (New York: Harper and Row, 1969).

17. Edward Rogers, *The Christian Approach to the Communist* (London: Edinburgh House, 1959), p. 8.

18. *World Christian Encyclopedia*, p. 6, For distributions by continents, see pp. 782-785.

19. *Religious Requirements and Practices of Certain Selected Groups* (Washington, D. C.: Department of the Army, 1980 Supplement), p. III-1.

20. *World Christian Encyclopedia*, pp. 6, 711.

21. Ibid., p. 837.

22. Ibid., p. 831. For distribution by continents, see pp. 782-785.

23. *U. S. News and World Report*, 88:13 (April 1980), p. 41.

24. Ibid., *World Christian Encyclopedia* p. 711.

25. Ibid., *World Christian Encyclopedia* p. 6.

26. *Religious Requirements and Practices of Certain Selected Groups: A Handbook for Chaplains* (Washington, D. C.: Department of the Army, 1978), p. IV-5.

27. Ibid., p. IV-17.

28. 1980 statistics for Confucianism: not quite 5 million. *World Christian Encyclopedia*, p. 6. WCE identifies Taoism with Chinese folk religion, with a world population of about 20 million Taoists. ibid., p. 846.

29. For an interesting discussion of these four religions with special attention to their American expressions, see Robert S. Ellwood, Jr., *The Eagle and the Rising Sun* (Philadelphia: Westminster Press, 1974).

30. Ellwood, *The Eagle*, p. 195.

31. *A Handbook for Chaplains*, p. IV-11. (See note 26 above).

32. Arnold J. Toynbee, "Encounters between Civilizations," *Civilizations on Trial* (New York: Oxford University Press, 1947), pp. 213-224. (First published in *Harper's Magazine*, April 1947).

5
Differing Missionary Responses to the New Era: Southern Baptists and United Methodists

How should the Christian churches of the United States respond to the new and exciting era which we have been discussing? We have already noted that the numbers of missionaries sent by the mainline American Protestant denominations have been decreasing for a number of years while those sent by the conservative wing of Protestantism have been increasing.

It may be instructive to compare and contrast the responses of two American denominational bodies, the Southern Baptist Convention and the United Methodist Church. My choice of these two may have been determined in part—at least subconsciously—by the fact that I am a Baptist and am greatly indebted to Methodists for nurturing me in my upbringing.

But there are better reasons for the selection. I suppose that both the Southern Baptist Convention and the United Methodist Church belong to that ambiguous category of "mainline" denominations. Of course these two are the largest Protestant denominational bodies in America. However, the United Methodist Church is strongly ecumenical, with membership in the National and World Councils of Churches, while the Southern Baptist Convention is neither affiliated with these councils nor with the interdenominational associations of conservative evangelicals, such as the National Association of Evangelicals and the World Evangelical Fellowship.

A Similar Pattern of Growth

In terms of their extensive growth and development in the history of the American republic, Baptists and Methodists are remarkably similar. Both were well adapted to the expansion of the nation on the westward-moving frontier. It is often remarked that the Baptists had a democratic church structure while the Methodists preached a democratic gospel. That is, the Baptists practiced congregational autonomy, which squared well with the spirit of freedom and individualism of the frontier, but they tended to hedge the gospel message about with Calvinistic overtones of the divine sovereignty and predestination which left the human will less than free. The Methodists, on the other hand, were far less democratic in their church polity but were Arminian in theology, giving strong emphasis to the freedom of the will to respond to the gospel.

Both Baptists and Methodists made ample use of revivalistic methods of evangelism. Likewise, both found solutions for the problems of providing a ministerial leadership for the frontier churches: the Baptists by ease of ordination, authorized by churches locally, and the Methodists by their remarkable system of lay leaders and circuit riders. Both ministered heroically on the frontier. It became common to say of miserable weather, "Today's not fit for anything to be out but crows and Methodist preachers."

When the United States came into being, the Congregationalists, Presbyterians, and Episcopalians were the largest religious groups in the nation, in that order, but by 1820 the Methodists and Baptists had moved into the two top places.[1] Both denominations were torn asunder by the slavery controversy. The Methodist Episcopal Church, South, was formed in 1844, and the Southern Baptist Convention a year later.

Methodists have been more successful than Baptists in healing the divisions which attended their early development in America. Baptists, with their emphasis upon individual freedom and responsibility, seem more inclined toward division than do Methodists. The Methodist Episcopal Church and the Methodist Episcopal Church, South, united in 1939, embracing also the small Methodist Protestant Church which had existed since 1832. The Methodist Church thus formed achieved a further union three decades later in 1968. It united with the Evangelical United Brethren Church, a church of similar doctrine and organization but with a German background, to form the United Methodist Church. The latter, with a membership of 9.4 million, includes most of the Methodists in the United States except for two or three predominantly black Methodist bodies.

The Southern Baptist Convention, on the other hand, has remained separate from the American Baptist Churches with which the southern congregations were originally united in one national structure.

The Southern Baptist Convention reports a total membership of 14.2 million.

Both the Baptists and Methodists have grown by winning the lower and middle classes. The Southern Baptist Convention and the United Methodist Church are great folk denominations, including the rank and file of Americans and therefore quite diverse in membership. The United Methodist Church has been unusually successful in including blacks within its membership. It is described by one of its leaders as sharing in the pluralism of American society more diverse now than ever before.[2] The Southern Baptist Convention also is a variegated body with a great increase of ethnic membership in recent years, including blacks, and with considerable theological, ideological and social diversity.

Clearly, the Southern Baptist Convention is not as ecumenically inclined as the United Methodist Church. However, the measure of Southern Baptist cooperation with other Christian bodies is often underestimated because it is less structured and therefore less visible. It is likely, also, that the United Methodist Church has considerably greater theological diversity than the Southern Baptist Convention.

The Development of International Missions:
Southern Baptist and Methodist

These two denominational bodies have carried on extensive international missions by means of significantly differing structures. The Southern Baptist Convention, throughout its existence, has operated home and foreign missions in separate organizations, a Home Mission Board and a Foreign Mission Board. Tasks of missionary education and cultivation are further distributed within the two Boards and beyond in the Woman's Missionary Union, the Brotherhood Commission, the Missions Education Council, and the Sunday School Board.

In the Methodist tradition, women's missionary societies have been sending agencies, which is not the case among Southern Baptists. In the United Methodist Church at present, overseas missions are the province of the World Division of the General Board of Global Ministries, a huge umbrella agency which includes also a National Division, a United Methodist Committee on Relief, a Women's Division, and divisions which have responsibility for missionary education and cultivation, personnel, etc.[3] Thus all that has to do with missions, national and international, comes under the aegis of one comprehensive board.

One other structural difference is significant. The Southern Baptist Convention, though it has spread to all fifty states of our nation, does not at this writing extend its connectional structures beyond our national boundaries. In international missionary work, although associations and conventions are formed, they are never structurally a part of the Southern Baptist Convention. Theoretically they are autonomous from the start, though actually they may remain under the tutelage of missionaries until they achieve a certain measure of development. The Southern Baptist Convention, therefore, is purely an American denominational body.

The Methodist structure is quite different. The United Methodist Church, through its international missions, develops churches which are organized into conferences which, in turn, have representation in the quadrennial General Conference, the supreme legislative body of the United Methodist Church. Thus the United Methodist Church is international in structure. Some of these overseas churches have had autonomous status for many decades, however, and by now the vast majority are autonomous. An autonomous church may still be "affiliated" with the United Methodist Church with the right to send nonvoting delegates to the General Conference. A further refinement by which these overseas conferences may go beyond affiliated status and have both autonomy and membership in the United Methodist Church is now under study.[4]

The missionary approaches of the Southern Baptists and Methodists have been quite similar. Both may be termed holistic or at least comprehensive. Various methods of evangelism and church development, including extensive publication enterprises and institutions for ministerial training, were combined with an array of social or community services, chief among which were education, medicine, and agriculture. The Methodist investment in these areas of social service has been considerably more extensive than that of Southern Baptists in proportion to the resources of the Methodists. It is probably true, however, that in absolute terms, Southern Baptists have invested more by means of their large budgets of recent years.

The overseas missionary work of both denominations developed about the same time. Although the Methodist Episcopal Church had some earlier, non-permanent mission work, its Missionary Society was not organized until 1819. The work in Liberia, which began in 1833, is regarded as "the first foreign mission of the Methodist Episcopal Church."[5] A mission was begun in South America in 1836, and in China in 1847.

The Foreign Mission Board of the Southern Baptist Convention was organized in 1845 along with the Convention itself. Previously, Baptist churches of the North and South had co-operated in the Baptist Triennial Convention since its organization in 1814 to support the work of the Adoniram Judsons in Burma. Missions in India and China had been added in 1836. The first missionaries of the Southern Baptist Foreign Mission Board were appointed for work in China in 1845 and the first missionaries to Africa the following year. Southern Baptists did not send missionaries to Burma and India though American (Northern) Baptists continued a strong work in those two countries.

The international missions of the Methodist Episcopal Church, larger than the Methodist Episcopal Church, South, formed by the slavery schism, developed much more rapidly than did those of Southern Baptists. No doubt the difficulties of the Reconstruction era in the South constituted a major factor in the tardiness of Southern Baptist development. By 1900, Southern Baptists, with 1.7 million members, had only 102 foreign missionaries for work in six countries. The Methodist Episcopal Church, with a membership of 2.7 million, had almost 900 foreign missionaries (see table 2 on p. 79).

At the quarter-century mark, Southern Baptists, having doubled in members in twenty-five years, had 528 missionaries working in thirteen countries. The Methodist Episcopal Church had 1925 missionaries for overseas work in twenty-nine countries. However, this large number could not be sustained because of financial stringencies due to overpledging of a Centenary program followed by the depression.[6] During the same time, Southern Baptists had a remarkably similar situation with regard to overpledging to a Seventy-Five Million (Dollar) Campaign. (See table 2, p. 79.)

The Postwar Period: Divergent Paths in Mission

By mid-century World War II was over, and the American missionary agencies were seeking to rebuild their international work which had been interrupted and greatly weakened—not to say devastated—by the war. The northern and southern branches of the Methodist

Table 2*

(UNITED) METHODIST CHURCH** OVERSEAS MISSIONS						
YEAR	MEMBER-SHIP METHOD-IST CHURCH	MISSION-ARIES SENT FROM US	COUN-TRIES	MEMBER-SHIP OVERSEAS	OVERSEAS MISSION BUDGET	OVERSEAS RELIEF BUDGET
1900	2.7 mil.	894	21	182,000	$ 1.7 mil.	
1925	4.5 mil.	1925	29	853,000	$ 5.5 mil.	
1948	8.5 mil.	1309	39	1 mil.	$ 6.4 mil.	
1958	9.5 mil.	1426	32	1.4 mil.	$14 mil. ($12 mil)	
1969	10.9 mil.	1397	36		$14.2 mil	$ 2.2 mil.
1975	10.1 mil.	788	32		$15.4 mil	$ 8 mil.
1983	9.4 mil.	617	55	4.2 mil.	$20.7 mil	$11.6 mil.

SOUTHERN BAPTIST CONVENTION OVERSEAS MISSIONS						
YEAR	MEMBER-SHIP SOU. BAPT. CONVEN-TION	MISSION-ARIES SENT FROM US	COUN-TRIES	MEMBER-SHIP OVERSEAS	OVERSEAS MISSION BUDGET	OVERSEAS RELIEF BUDGET
1900	1.7 mil.	102	6	7,000	$202,000	
1925	3.6 mil.	528	13	140,000	$ 3.5 mil.	
1948	6.3 mil.	670	25	162,000	$ 5.1 mil.	
1958	9.0 mil.	1283	29	417,000	$15.5 mil.	
1969	11.3 mil.	2564	70	631,000	$31.0 mil	
1975	12.5 mil.	2667	78	896,000	$46.8 mil	$ 1.7 mil.
1983	14.2 mil.	3346	102	1.7 mil.	$110.5 mil	$ 7.2 mil.

(* Statistics derived from sources too numerous to list.)
(** (United) Methodist Church statistics are as follows: 1900 and 1925, Methodist Episcopal Church—not including M.E. Church, South; 1948 and 1958, Methodist Church (organized in 1939); 1969 and after, United Methodist Church (formed in 1968).)

Episcopal Church along with the smaller Methodist Protestant Church had united in 1939 to form the Methodist Church, the largest Protestant body in the United States, with over 8.5 million members in 1948. Southern Baptist membership had increased dramatically to 6.3 million in 1948.

Programs of "Advance"

In this same year, 1948, both the Methodist Church and the Southern Baptist Convention adopted programs of "Advance" calling for greatly increased giving for missions and rehabilitation of overseas work and accelerated appointments of missionary personnel. At this time, the Methodist Church was still far ahead of Southern Baptists in numbers of overseas missionaries, about 1300 to 670.

The Advance program of Southern Baptists resulted in much greater statistical increases than that of the Methodist Church. One factor in this growth was the strategic and widespread deployment of China missionaries to begin Southern Baptist work in other countries of East and Southeast Asia after the closing of China to foreign missions in 1949.

After two decades, in 1969, Southern Baptists had nearly twice as many overseas missionaries as the newly formed United Methodist Church—2564 to 1397—in about twice as many countries—seventy to thirty-six. Baptist overseas appropriations in this year amounted to more than twice those of United Methodists. Also, during this crucial span of two decades, the Southern Baptist Convention had almost doubled its membership to displace the United Methodist Church as the largest Protestant body in America.

Southern Baptists: "Bold Mission Thrust"

From 1969 to the present, the Southern Baptist increase in overseas missions has continued unabated. At the end of 1983, the Foreign Mission Board had 3346 missionaries under appointment for 102 countries, including 232 short-term personnel. The 1983 budget for overseas work was $110.5 million, and the Foreign Mission Board channeled $7.2 million of relief funds overseas in 1983.

This huge increase was undergirded by a "Bold Mission Thrust" program adopted by the Southern Baptist Convention in 1976. The aim of Bold Mission Thrust is that by the efforts of Southern Baptists along with other Christians, everybody in the world will have heard the gospel message by AD 2000. Specific goals for the Foreign Mission Board include more than 5000 missionaries at work in 125 countries by the year 2000. While the central emphasis is upon career missionaries, there is an accelerated effort to involve many lay volunteers in short-term assignments, as many as 10,000 per year by the end of the century. Also included is a goal of multiplying the number of overseas churches tenfold with concomitant increases in baptisms and church membership.[7]

During the postwar period, the financial support of the spectacular expansion of Southern Baptist foreign missionary work has been provided primarily from two sources: a unified financial system called the "Cooperative Program," which undergirds all Southern Baptist agencies, and a special offering gathered each year between Thanksgiving and Christmas. This "Lottie Moon" Christmas Offering is named for Charlotte ("Lottie") Digges Moon (1840-1912), a China missionary of the Southern Baptist Foreign Mission Board noted for her sacrificial manner of life. In 1887, Miss Moon advocated a season of prayer and giving for foreign missions and urged Baptist women's organizations to sponsor the idea. Interestingly enough, her suggestion was inspired by the example of Methodist women who had decided to observe the week before Christmas, 1887, as a time of prayer and self-denial for missions.[8]

This offering has grown to amazing proportions. In 1983, it amounted to over $58 million.[9] Each year it sets a new record as the largest single offering for foreign missions in history.

Obviously, Southern Baptists are well on the way to their goal of over 5000 missionaries in 125 countries by the year 2000. At the end of 1983, as we have noted, with seventeen years yet to go, there were 3346 missionaries at work in 102 countries.

What is responsible for this Southern Baptist missionary dynamism? A perceptive Southern Baptist has remarked that from their earliest beginnings "there has not been a moment . . . that Baptists in the South have not been concerned about the next hill, the next valley, the next state, the next nation, the next continent even unto the uttermost."[10] This missionary zeal, insofar as international missions are concerned, has been especially marked since World War II.

To be sure, such a missionary mentality could be viewed as no more than a denominational triumphalism or imperialism. It is not the purpose of this book to probe the psychological and sociological

E. Stanley Jones,
Methodist missionary to India

M. Theron Rankin,
Executive Secretary, Foreign
Mission Board, SBC, 1945-53

Baker James Cauthen,
Executive Secretary, Foreign
Mission Board, SBC, 1954-79

R. Keith Parks,
President, Foreign Mission
Board, SBC, 1980-.

motivations of Southern Baptists. No doubt one could document relationships of Southern regionalism and Southern Baptist denominational consciousness, the forging of a confidence in the superior efficiency of Southern Baptist methods and programs, etc. Especially during the early postwar years and through the 1950s, Southern Baptist denominational rhetoric was sometimes strident and given to exaggerated claims.[11]

This kind of rhetoric, fortunately, has become exceptional and there are indications of a more mature denominational awareness and a wholesome respect for Christians of other persuasions. Or at least, so it appears to me. There are hosts of Southern Baptist people who are genuinely committed to missions because they are deeply committed to Jesus Christ and to the biblical revelation as they understand it. They sincerely wish to share their faith because their faith has profound meaning for them personally.

Nor should the factor of able, inspiring leadership be overlooked. A succession of chief executives of the Southern Baptist Foreign Mission Board, M. Theron Rankin, 1945-1953, Baker J. Cauthen, 1954-19p, and R. Keith Parks, since 1980, in concert with several other denominational leaders, have helped fuel the fires of missionary dynamism.

This tidal wave of Southern Baptist missionary expansion shows little sign of receding except as it is threatened by the internecine conflicts, power struggles, and pressures toward theological conformity which have erupted with new strength and in new forms in recent years.

United Methodists: Retrenchment in Overseas Missions

Unlike the Southern Baptists, the United Methodists did not sustain the program of Advance adopted in 1948—at least in terms of the usual measurements of missionary advance: increased budgetary commitments, number of missionaries, etc. As the table on page 79 indicates, 1958 registers an increase in missionaries sent by the Methodist Church, but 1969 shows a decrease in spite of the fact that the union by which the United Methodist Church was formed in 1968 added 145 Evangelical United Brethren missionaries to the roster.[12]

Then followed a serious reduction of overseas missionaries from 1397 in 1969 to only 617 by 1983. The number of overseas nationals supported as "persons in mission" by no means compensated for this decrease.

It appears that this retrenchment was not the result of a deliberately devised policy. More than once leaders of the World Division of the General Board of Global Ministries of the United Methodist Church affirmed the validity of sending missionaries.

For example, in 1973 when United Methodists were suffering the effects of financial stringencies due to inflation, dollar devaluation, and declining membership, one of the executives of the World Division of the Board of Global Ministries reiterated the division's evaluation of the significance of the missionary: "We affirm the validity of the missionary presence as an essential part of the Gospel. . . . We believe the place of persons at the heart of mission to be an abiding reality." But he indicated, also, that "the sending of missionaries can no longer be considered a monopoly of Western churches," and that many Christians of Asia, Latin America, and Africa are eminently better qualified to execute mission than are persons from the West. The number of missionaries is important, he said, but it is not the sole criterion for measuring the effectiveness of the World Division.[13]

Four years later, 1977, another executive of the World Division declared: "This is no time to conclude that retrenchment in world mission is the order of the day for the United Methodist Church. The challenge and responsibility for world mission is too great for this."[14] There were continuing efforts to step up the recruitment of missionaries, both in terms of those sent from the United States and overseas nationals supported as "persons in mission."[15]

Yet the overall record is one of quite striking reductions in overseas personnel. Why this significant decrease? The reasons given by representatives of the World Division are similar to those we have suggested for the general retrenchment of mainline denominations (see p. 31).

Charles H. Germany, for several years an executive of the World Division, noted certain political realities—the closing of some fields such as China, North Korea, and Burma; difficulties in procuring visas for India, Malaysia, and Indonesia; and changing circumstances in other countries such as Rhodesia (now Zimbabwe) and Zaire— which made the missionary presence problematical.

But he stressed the coming of age of the "colleague churches" with which the Methodist missionaries worked. The old era of dependence has ended, Germany said, and the church is now clearly in control of its life and ministry in every country to which the World Division is related. There is a heightened determination to see trained nationals in places of responsibility in the church, he noted, and these changes "have brought 'career anxiety' to many missionaries, resulting in a high rate of attrition." Germany predicted that conservative evangelicals also would find themselves at the end of an era when their colleague churches came to the point of self-determination.[16]

In addition, missionary administrators of the United Methodist Church noted realistically that reduced finances, inflation, and dollar devaluation during the 1970s played havoc with budgets of the World Division.[17]

Stress was placed, also, upon the internationalizing of missions. We have already alluded to the fact that the World Division, in addition to its roster of missionaries who were United States citizens, was supporting a number of persons who were members of colleague churches working in their own countries or abroad. In 1979 there were 246 of these "persons in mission" from Asia, Africa, Europe, the Caribbean, and Latin America.[18] These greatly extended the countries where the World Division was involved as well, so that in 1981 the number was more than ninety.[19]

Some of these overseas persons in mission were welcomed here in this country. In 1980, the officials of the Board of Global Ministries were recounting the blessings of receiving as well as sending missionaries: "When missionaries come out of the liberating struggles of Africa, they share a faith which has been through the fire," they said. "When missionaries come out of the Korean struggle for human rights, they share a faith that has escaped prison bars. When missionaries come from the streets of Calcutta, they share a faith which has slept with the outcasts." They concluded that "we can no longer claim to have a complete understanding of the faith when these have so much to teach us."[20]

In 1982, J. Harry Haines, long associated with the world mission and world relief outreach of the United Methodist Church reported the results of a questionnaire circulated among 150 persons widely representative of the membership of this church. In the responses some "blocks . . . that prevent evangelism and growth" and "inhibit mission and social concerns" were suggested. Among these were the lack of a singleness of purpose, and theological uncertainty, especially at the point of the complex question of God's presence and revelation among persons of other religions.[21]

A question concerning the future of mission, evangelism, and social concern elicited conflicting opinions about missionary involvement. Some called for more commitment to mission in this country but only indirect involvement internationally. Others felt that there needed to be a reassessment of present missionary priorities of the United Methodist Church—whether there should only be assistance to overseas churches, "or whether indeed there are many open doors in the unevangelized areas of the world that we simply refuse to enter."[22]

Some Summary Reflections

Now let me offer by way of summary some reflections upon the quite different responses of Southern Baptists and United Methodists to the postwar missionary situation.

Differing Stages of Missionary Development

The Methodist missionary work in 1948 was not only more extensive than that of Southern Baptists—thirty-nine countries compared to twenty-five—but was also much older and more highly developed in most places. This was largely because the early strength of Methodists was predominantly north of the Mason-Dixon line and therefore not so greatly affected by the struggle for reconstruction in the South following the Civil War.

In part, also, this higher level of development was due to the fact that the prominent Methodist bodies had mutually cooperated in their overseas missionary work, seeking to develop in a given country one Methodist constituency. Southern and Northern Baptists, while cooperating, did not usually have work in the same countries. In cases where they did, such as China and Japan, they did not consistently develop united conventions.

In any case, membership statistics show clearly the contrast in numerical strength. In 1948 the overseas churches of the Methodist Church had more than a million members, while those related to Southern Baptists had only 162,000. Even when allowance is made for the inclusion of "preparatory members" and baptized children in the Methodist figures, the disparity is rather striking. The Methodists were relating to older, larger, and presumably stronger and more mature, colleague churches than were the Southern Baptists. Hence the Methodist sensitivity to the need to emphasize the leadership and initiative of their colleague churches seems quite appropriate. Notice also that during this period of reduced missionary personnel, the overseas Methodist churches continued to grow significantly. In 1983 they reported 4.2 million members, compared to 1.7 million members of churches related to Southern Baptist overseas missions (see table on pp.79).

Diffusion of United Methodist Priorities

There was some redirection of the energies and resources of the Methodists after 1948. We have already noted the attempt at a greater internationalizing of missions by supporting overseas nationals as "persons in mission" beginning in the early 1970s. But there were other important ways of redirection.

The Methodists sustained a larger and more continuous program of world relief and development after 1948 than did Southern Baptists. While both had special offerings and rather extensive programs of relief and rehabilitation in the early postwar years, the Methodist Church has had a special committee existing since 1940 and continuing to the present as the United Methodist Committee on Relief (UMCOR). This committee, operating within the larger structure of Methodist missionary organization, was spending over $2 million annually in the 1960s in extensive relief and development programs overseas. In the 1970s and 80s its budget was vastly increased, during the very period which saw reductions in the overseas missionary personnel and budgets of the World Division. UMCOR'S spending increased from $2.2 million in 1969 to $11.6 million in 1983.

The Southern Baptist Foreign Mission Board did not begin a large, continuing relief program until 1975 though some Southern Baptist contributions had gone to the world relief program of the Baptist World Alliance. By the 1980s, a significant and diversified relief and development program was being executed by the Foreign Mission Board. The 1983 outlay was $7.2 million.

The Methodists also directed some attention to difficult issues related to missions and missionary organization. In 1973, for example, the Board of Managers of the Board of Global Ministries of the United Methodist Church decided upon the following goals for the Board of Global Ministries and its units—including, of course, the World Division—for the next biennium:

—articulation and proclamation of the Gospel leading persons to Christian commitment;

—elimination of racism and sexism leading to liberation and empowerment;

—alleviation of human need, and response to threats against global survival;

—development and strengthening of congregations and institutions as centers of Christian worship and mission;

—reflection on the oneness of Christ's church and interdependence of all the world's people.[23]

At the same time with regard to the issue of sexism the Board of Global Ministries reported that it had complied with the mandate of the General Conference that 40 percent of the top executives of the Board should be women.[24]

The above is not the only allusion to liberation struggles to be found in the reports of the Board of Global Ministries. The World Division has continued to give priority to such programs as "Ministries of Human Freedom and Justice" along with "Calling to Discipleship" and "Leadership Development."[25] No doubt the strong black presence within the United Methodist Church has influenced its emphasis upon racial justice in this country and abroad.

Much of the denominational energy was directed to ecumenical interests and involvements. Not only was there cooperation in the National and World Council of Churches and the Consultation on Church Union (COCU) after its development in the early 1960s. There was also the process which resulted in the formation of The United Methodist Church in 1968. In a little more than forty years The United Methodist Church has integrated together seven denominations in one. To bring together and amalgamate the various denominational agencies undoubtedly took an inordinate amount of thought and energy and spawned a host of problems.[26]

I believe it is fair to say that the Southern Baptist Foreign Mission Board has sustained much more of a unified focus upon missions in the more traditional sense than has the World Division of United Methodists: the sending of missionaries, the development of indigenous churches and ministries to human need.

In 1976, the Foreign Mission Board issued a "Special Report to the Southern Baptist Convention," which included a carefully crafted statement of "Basic Principles" along with a summary of goals for the new program of "Bold Mission Thrust." Two of the "Basic Principles" are of special relevance to this singleness of purpose to which I have just alluded:

—Missionaries go to their fields to share the gospel of Christ and minister to human need. They do not involve themselves in political or commercial affairs. They are recognized as people who are dedicated to the purpose of Christian witness and service. Anything that will make unclear that image will greatly handicap their efforts, and, in some places, make impossible their residence in the country. . . .

—Evangelism and church development will be maintained as the imperatively central thrusts. Compassionate ministries are no less insistent as expressions of obedience and examples of Christian compassion in action.[27]

The goals of Bold Mission Thrust, likewise, were consistent with these "central thrusts":[28] evangelism, church development, and ministries of compassion.

While the Foreign Mission Board through its executive staff as well as some of its missionaries has spoken out from time to time on racism in American society, it has tended to be aloof toward liberation struggles abroad in keeping with the policy of political neutrality expressed above. It has hardly begun to address the thorny but important issue of the role of women in Christian ministry.

As to ecumenism the Southern Baptist Convention, including its Foreign Mission Board, has become more cooperative with other Christians in recent years but has remained unaffiliated with the major structures of ecumenism. Thus one sees much more of a diffusion of missionary priorities in the overseas ministries of the United Methodist Church than in those of the Southern Baptist Convention.

Problems of Identity

Statistically, the Southern Baptist Convention, with some nervous wavering from time to time, has sustained a remarkable growth during this century. Church membership considerably more than tripled during the half-century, 1900-1948, and significantly more than doubled during the next thirty-five years, 1948-1983.

Methodist growth, on the other hand, recorded a rapid surge during the nineteenth century and a significant increase in this century until the early 1970s, when it reached a peak and started to decline. Some Methodists, in response to the questionnaire previously discussed, insisted that the diminishing of commitment to missions, especially as indicated by decreased financial support, was inseparably related to this loss in membership.[29] The relation of cause and effect may be difficult to determine.

J. Harry Haines suggested that the greatly increased diversity within the United Methodist Church, reflecting the dramatic changes in American population patterns, may have provoked something of an identity crisis,[30] a judgment supported by more recent research by United Methodists.[31] While Southern Baptist zeal seems fairly constant, growing diversity has had its effects and identity problems are by no means absent. Who are the "true" Southern Baptists, for example, when it comes to questions of biblical interpretation, theological conformity, school prayer, and other issues?

Early in 1984, dissatisfaction with the General Board of Global Ministries, only mildly represented in the report of the questionnaire, erupted divisively. Some conservatives and moderates took action to organize a rival agency in Atlanta, The Mission Society for United Methodists. They expressed their intention to send missionaries in response to requests from colleague churches abroad, as well as send missionaries to areas where churches do not exist.[32]

However, strong opposition to the organization of this new agency emerged among bishops and district superintendents.

Then in May, 1984, the General Conference of the United Methodist Church supported, by a slim margin, the Board of Global Ministries as the sole missions agency of the church but called upon its officers to be more responsible. They also voted to fund a four-year study of missions.[33]

The General Conference also reaffirmed both evangelism and social justice. They made plans to reach ethnic minorities, especially the immigrant communities of Koreans and Hispanics in the United States. And they set a bold goal of twenty million members by 1992! At the same time, new initiatives for peace and justice were called for. Deep concern for the poor and oppressed was expressed. And the bishops, through their episcopal address, issued the strongest statement on peace yet put forth by any group of church leaders in America. They called for the renunciation not only of nuclear but also of conventional weapons.[34]

Conclusion

We have traced the divergent responses to the postwar missionary situation on the part of the two largest Protestant denominational bodies in the United States. Of course being one of the biggest by no means guarantees that a denomination is the most important to the cause of Christ and his kingdom. But ampler resources of personnel and money surely mean larger responsibilities.

Since 1948, and especially since 1969, these two denominational giants have followed somewhat divergent paths in interpreting and fulfilling their missionary responsibilities. There is room for differing judgments as to which of the two paths is more nearly Christian. But surely there is room also, within the universal Christian fellowship, for denominations which interpret their Christian tasks differently.

From my own perspective, I commend United Methodists for their attention to fundamental human issues as well as their concern for the selfhood of the overseas churches. At the same time, along with critics within the United Methodist Church, I am compelled to raise questions about their failure to enter open doors to unevangelized areas in the postwar period.

Conversely, United Methodists have a right to raise questions with me about the meaning of my own denomination's missionary expansion at home and abroad: to what degree it is motivated by a Southern Baptist imperialism, whether it is adequately sensitive to the selfhood of churches and whether it is sufficiently balanced by a vital concern for basic human issues.

Let us hope that in fellowship and cooperation not only Baptists and Methodists but Christians of all denominations and all nations will mutually encourage and correct each other for the edification of all and the advance of Christ's kingdom.

Notes

1. Arthur Carl Piephorn, *Profiles in Belief: the Religious Bodies of the United States and Canada*, vol. II (New York: Harper and Row, 1978), p. 570.

2. J. Harry Haines, *Committed Locally, Living Globally* (Nashville: Abingdon, 1982), p. 13.

3. Jack M. Tuell, *The Organization of the United Methodist Church*, rev. ed. (Nashville: Abingdon, 1982), pp. 138-141.

4. Ibid., p. 118.

5. Thomas Benjamin Neely, *The Methodist Episcopal Church and Its Foreign Missions* (New York: Methodist Book Concern, 1923), p. 71.

6. *Report of the Executive Secretary of the Division of Foreign Missions to the Methodist Annual Meeting, Dec. 7-10, 1948* (New York: Board of Missions and Church Extension of the Methodist Church, 1948), p. 31.

7. *The Commission*, 39:6 (June 1976), p. 3.

8. Catherine B. Allen, *The New Lottie Moon Story* (Nashville: Broadman Press, 1980), pp. 169-170.

9. Baptist Press, June 5, 1984.

10. Albert McClellan, cited in John R. Cheyne, *The Imperative Impulse* (Nashville: Convention Press, 1983), p. 12.

11. See E. Luther Copeland, "The Ecumenical Movement: Will Southern Baptists Ever Get With It?" *Perspectives in Religious Studies*, 11:1 (Spring 1975), pp. 21-22.

12. *Journal of the General Conference, United Methodist Church*, 1968, p. 1648.

13. John F. Schaefer, in United Methodist Church, Board of Global Ministries, *Journal of the Second Annual Meeting*, October 19-27, 1973, pp. 460-462.

14. Charles H. Germany, in *New World Outlook*, 37:1 (September 1977), p. 26.

15. Ibid.; also Lois C. Miller, in ibid., 38:8 (April 1978), p. 10.

16. Germany, *New World Outlook*, pp. 24-25.

17. Schaefer, *Journal of the Second Annual Meeting;* also *New World Outlook*, 39:7 (April 1979), p. 33.

18. *New World Outlook*, 40:8 (April 1980), p. 13.

19. *Ibid.*, 41:8 (April 1981), p. 14.

20. Frederick Wertz and Tracey K. Jones, Jr., "Our Mission Today," *New World Outlook*, 40:7 (March 1980), p. 11.

21. J. Harry Haines, *Committed Locally, Living Globally* pp. 58-59.

22. Ibid., pp. 61-62.

23. *New World Outlook*, 34:8 (April 1973), p. 12.

24. Ibid.

25. *New World Outlook*, 43:8 (April 1983), pp. 9-14.

26. Kristine M. Rogers and Bruce A. Rogers, *Paths to Transformation, A Study of the General Agencies of the United Methodist Church* (Nashville: Abingdon, 1982), pp. 24-32.

27. Foreign Mission Board, "One Hundred and Thirty-First Annual Report," *Southern Baptist Convention Annual*, 1976, p. 112.

28. Ibid., pp. 112-113.

29. Haines, *Committed Locally, Living Globally*, p. 56.

30. Ibid., p. 13.

31. See Elliott Wright, "Weak Ecclesiology and Donatism," *The Christian Century*, 101:19 (May 30 1984), p. 564.

32. *Time*, 123:5 (January 30 1984), p. 71; *Christianity Today*, 28:2 (February 3 1984), p. 64.

33. *News and Observer*, May 20 1984, p. 7D.

34. Wright, "Weak Ecclesiology and Donatism."

6
American Missionaries
in a Postcolonial World

The chapter immediately preceding implied a sanction upon the sending of missionaries from the United States into the non-Western world. But we need to face this issue more forthrightly: Should we continue to send American missionaries into the Third World in a postcolonial era? Can they function effectively? Of course, the same question may be asked concerning missionaries from any of the Western nations and even from Japan, since Japan has had colonies and is now associated with the economic powers which dominate the Third World.

However, I want to focus upon the problem of American missionaries because I am an American, because the vast majority of Protestant missionaries sent are Americans, and because Americans may have special advantages or handicaps in addressing the gospel to Third World peoples.

The problem we have raised has several facets. Let us try and clarify the issue before attempting an answer.

The Memory of the Colonial Past

The question of the appropriateness of sending American missionaries into the Third World has to do first of all with the colonial past. As we have noticed, from the 1490s until after World War II, Christian missions, both Catholic and Protestant, operated in a world dominated by the imperialistic outreach of Western powers. The missions were often identified as but the religious arm of the vast imperialistic and colonial enterprise.

This charge was most consistently and clamantly made in China during and after the Communist revolution. Chinese Christians were labeled "running dogs of the imperialists." Missionaries were expelled, the Chinese churches were reorganized independent from the

Western churches which had planted them, and the flow of Western missionary personnel and money into China was barred.

But the same charge has echoed from many places in the Third World. An Indonesian pastor and missionary to the United States has reminded us that "Christianity in Muslim eyes is identical with foreign imperialism, forcing its religious system as well as its economic (system) on other people." And he quotes a Muslim, a former Prime Minister of Indonesia, as follows: "The whites . . . first . . . sent their missionaries, then their mercenaries, and finally their military. We call these the 'Three M's' of imperialism."[1]

A Latin American theologian says, "We have discovered that the missionary enterprise of the last one hundred and fifty years is closely related to and interwoven with the expansion of the economic, political, and cultural influence of the Anglo-Saxon world."[2] A Filipino churchman states that the image of the missionary as seen by the younger generation in the Third World is not a symbol of "the authenticity of the Gospel and the universality of the Church" but rather "a symbol of the unversality of Western imperialism."[3]

A Christian writer concerned with communicating the gospel in the Third World, who identifies himself as a former Buddhist, puts it even more emphatically:

> Christianity came to most of the Third World, not as a message of salvation and liberation but as a concomitant to captivity and enslavement. The great empire builders . . . brought Christianity as a part of the package of 'civilization' that they bestowed upon the 'natives.' . . . And Christianity, as an institution, is still identified as having been, after the army and the police, the most powerful weapon in the arsenal of the oppressor. Whether Christianity actually served in such a capacity can, I suppose, be debated. But . . . in the minds of vast multitudes who are the 'beneficiaries' of the colonial experience, this is not a matter for debate. For them it is a fact of their traumatic history.[4]

In this situation, where the memory of the colonial past is vivid, does the American missionary have any advantage over missionaries from other Western countries? After all, our nation began with an anticolonial revolution; often we have been critical of Western colonialism, and our own colonialism in the Caribbean and the Pacific came late and was at least euphemistically described as "liberation" of colonials from the oppressive Spanish yoke.

Undoubtedly, there is some reservoir of appreciation of our having rebelled against the foreign rule of the British and especially our experiment with democratic government and our forging of a pluralistic society. I certainly found this to be the case in my sojourn in India in the 1960s. To a lesser degree, I found that the Japanese admired the American experiment and the American dream. Certainly in much of the world, there is a broad perception of Americans as champions of human rights though this image is too often effaced by the spectacle of the "ugly American" abroad, the violence of American society, and the ambiguity of the influence of the human rights issue in American foreign policy.

By and large, however, little distinction is made between Americans and "other Europeans" in this memory of the colonial past. If former subjects of the far-flung British Empire in the Third World identify with us in our having achieved independence from the British, they are not unaware of the history of our internal colonialism: the subjugation of blacks and native Americans in our society.

The Perception of the Imperialistic Present

Even if we grant that Americans have some advantage in our less-than-complete identification with the colonial masters of the past, surely the reverse is true in the awareness of present imperialism. And it is this latter which seems of more immediate concern to many Third World persons. They believe themselves to be victims of international systems of economic and political dominance in which the powerful nations conspire with elites in the developing countries to keep the masses in poverty and economic bondage. The United States is viewed by some as the chief perpetrator of this neo-imperialism.

Orlando Costas, a prominent missiologist, native of Puerto Rico and identified with Latin America, sees the present misery of the masses of that large area of the Third World as inherent in the fact that the economy from the beginning

was structured for the advantage of the European metropolis (represented during the first three centuries by Spain and Portugal, but later by Great Britain and the United States . . .). As such, Latin America has been incorporated into the world economy to provide two things— raw materials and cheap labor. This has left not only an exploited continent, but also one that is dominated by the economic policies of the new economic metropolis (Western Europe, North America, and

Japan), oppressed by governments and national oligarchies allied with the former and multinational corporations, and dependent upon the goodwill of the international market.[5]

More broadly, Costas, while admitting that Western technology has made certain important contributions to world society, charges it with enabling "Western societies (and particularly the United States) ... to dominate, domesticate, and oppress less-developed societies."[6] Costas, along with many others, identifies the "non-White" minorities of the United States ("Blacks, Hispanics, Native Americans, and Asians") with the exploited peoples of the Third World.[7]

In articulating this charge of economic imperialism, a Filipino Catholic layman makes a poignant indictment of the betrayal of the American dream:

> Global justice ... is bread and freedom for all in the world and it is no different from the original American Dream for all Americans. ... Both the extremes of fascism and communism believe that freedom must go in favor of bread and order. The American Dream once believed they could and should go together. But now with poverty amid plenty on her own soil, America stands charged with the opposite indictment—that she is fostering the sacrifice of other people's freedom for bread—bread, to use the current colloquialism, for the pocketbooks of U. S. stockholders.[8]

American missionaries, therefore, must reckon with the perception of many people in the Third World that the United States is the major villian in the neo-imperialism which exploits them and keeps them poverty-stricken and impotent.

Concern for the Selfhood of the Young Churches

The question of whether American missionaries can function effectively in the Third World has also to do with the independence of the young churches which have for the most part been planted and nurtured by missionaries from the West. The issue here is in no way unique to missions from the United States compared to those from other countries except that the vast majority of missionaries and monies, so far as Protestant missions are concerned, comes from the United States.

It is to this issue primarily that the call for "Moratorium" was addressed in the 1970s. This call, articulated by certain African church leaders and then joined by some church leaders from other areas of the Third World, proposed that a moratorium of a few years be declared during which foreign missionaries be withdrawn. The chief spokesman was John Gatu, General Secretary of the Presbyterian Church of East Africa. Mr. Gatu's basic argument was "that the churches of the Third World must be allowed to find their own identity, and that the continuation of the present missionary movement is a hindrance to this selfhood of the church."[9]

Although the call for moratorium itself was never more than a minority voice, undoubtedly the concern for the selfhood of the young churches is well nigh universal in the Christianity of the Third World.

Affluent Missionaries Among the Poor

Another difficult facet of the problem of sending American missionaries to the Third World is the fact that the American missionaries represent affluence whereas the majority of Third World people are poor. Again, if American missionaries are to be differentiated from other Western missionaries in this regard, it is because there are more of them and on the whole they have more money at their disposal.

Perhaps most missionaries are surprised to find themselves considered affluent. I remember the shock of discovering that my family and I were looked upon as wealthy in Japan in the early postwar period when Japan's economy was prostrate and many Japanese were suffering severe deprivation. A comfortable Western-style house, plenty to eat, access to an automobile (shared with one or two other missionary families), reasonably good clothes—all of these were marks of wealth. It mattered little that the house and the automobile did not belong to us personally but were mission property. Poverty and wealth, of course, are relative matters. Though I had grown up as one of the Appalachian poor, in Japan in the early 1950s living on a very modest missionary salary, I was wealthy! Japan today is quite another matter.

The missionary from the United States is a rich person in most of the Third World. Can she or he function effectively as an ambassador of Christ in those circumstances?

The "Spiritual Bankruptcy" of the West

People of the Third World are often appalled by the loose sexual morality, the ease and frequency of divorce, the shocking crime rate, and the prevalence of violence in Western countries and especially the

United States. American missionaries abroad are sometimes embarrassed when their colleagues or acquaintances visit the United States
only to be victimized by crime, especially by the theft of money or
other belongings. The question arises whether an apparently decadent
culture can any longer be the base from which missionaries of a
life-transforming gospel can be sent. Is not the contradiction too
overwhelming, it is asked.

A Third World Christian states that the cultures of the West

> are seen by most Third World societies as being an embodiment of
> values that are mostly contrary to the Gospel message. While the
> Gospel promises salvation in Christ and a release from our 'Adamic'
> selves, the Third World sees Christendom as being built upon some of
> the worst characteristics of Adam in man—individualism, acquisitive-
> ness, greed, conflict, exploitation, oppression and war. Behind the tinsel
> niceties and superficial 'liberalism' of western civilization, the Third
> World tends to perceive what it believes to be its true nature—a ruth-
> less and insatiable acquisitiveness and a readiness to throw its 'Chris-
> tian' pretensions to the winds when the life-styles built upon
> acquisitiveness and greed are seriously threatened. It tends to see a
> congruence between the affluence of Christendom and the sins that
> Jesus preached against.[10]

So this is the problem: all things considered—involvement in imperialism past and present, concern for the selfhood of the young
churches, the contrasts of affluence and poverty, the alleged spiritual
bankruptcy of the West—should we continue to send missionaries
from the United States and other Western countries into the Third
World?

Some Suggested Answers

Many answers are given to this question, and not a few are negative.
To be sure, some governments of non-Western countries have answered in the negative by disallowing or placing severe restrictions on
the entrance of missionaries from the West. I am especially concerned
here, however, with the responses of Christians both in the Third
World and in the United States.

A Qualified "No"

Those church leaders of the Third World associated with the call
for moratorium were giving a qualified negative answer to the ques-

tion of whether American and other Western missionaries should continue to be sent to the non-Western world. They were asking for the suspension of missionary help for a time. In John Gatu's case, he first suggested a moratorium of not less than five years. He later said that "missionaries should be withdrawn, period" in order not to impose a timetable upon God. Even so, he seems not to have envisioned a permanent withdrawal.[11]

The moratorium debate has long since subsided. Perhaps the opportunity to vent feelings about the necessity of identity and selfhood was itself salutary. David Stowe's remark seems to be to the point, namely, that these "fierce arguments" of the 1970s "were really about colonialism, and colonialism has no defenders today (even though some practitioners may remain)."[12] The call for moratorium was a clamant cry for local independence and the end of paternalistic, imperialistic missionary attitudes and practices.

I suggest also that the serious reductions of missionary personnel and money by the mainline denominations may be considered a qualified "no" to the question which this chapter addresses. At least, the representatives of these agencies have considered it ill-advised to continue sending a large stream of American missionaries and funds into the areas of the Third World churches. We have noticed that a prime motivation in this retrenchment is precisely the sensitivity concerning the needs for identity and selfhood on the part of the young church which the proponents of moratorium articulated. Whether there has been an adequate concern for the millions yet unevangelized is another question.

A Qualified "Yes"

The vast majority of the leaders of Third World churches did not identify with the call for moratorium. They acquiesced in the continued sending of missionaries from the West, but under certain conditions. Their answer, then, is a qualified affirmative.

Perhaps none has spoken more eloquently to this issue than Bishop Federico Pagura of Argentina. Following is the English translation of a statement he read to a meeting of Costa Ricans and missionaries when he was bishop of the United Methodist Church of Costa Rica and Panama:

Missionary, go home . . . or stay.

If you are not able to separate the eternal Word of the Gospel from the cultural molds in which you carried it to these lands and taught it with genuine abnegation: Missionary, go home.

If you are not able to identify with the events, anxieties, and aspirations of those people prematurely aged by an unequal struggle which seems to have neither termination nor hope: Missionary, go home.

If your allegiance and fidelity to your nation of origin are stronger than loyalty and obedience to Jesus Christ who came "to put down the mighty and lift up the lowly" (Luke 1:52): Missionary, go home.

If you are not able to love and respect as equals those whom you once came to evangelize as "the lost": Missionary, go home.

If you are not able to rejoice at the entry of new peoples and churches upon a new stage of maturity, independence, and responsibility, even at the price of committing errors like you and your compatriots committed also in the past: Missionary, go home.

For it is time to go home.

But if you are ready to bear the risks and pains of this hour of birth which our American peoples are experiencing, even denying yourself, if you begin to celebrate with them the happiness of sensing that the Gospel is not only proclamation and affirmation of a distant hope but of a hope and liberation which are already transforming history, if you are ready to give more of your time, your values, your life in the service of these peoples who are awaking, then:

STAY! There is much to do; hands and blood are lacking for an undertaking so immense in which Christ is the protagonist and pioneer.[13]

It is clear that those American sending agencies, mostly in the conservative evangelical or independent categories, which continue to send missionaries into the Third World without serious numerical reductions—or in increasing numbers—are giving an affirmative answer to our question. I should think that none of them gives an unqualified yes. Surely most of the leaders of these agencies have some sensitivity to the feelings and attitudes of Third World Christians concerning missions and colonialism, the selfhood of churches, etc.

Nevertheless, there is cause for concern that the mainline denominations, with long experience in relating to the Third World, have greatly diminished their missionary personnel while newer, less-experienced agencies—sometimes without well-defined requirements or adequate orientation for their missionaries—have entered heavily into the missionary movement from the United States. Wilbert Shenk, a Mennonite missionary executive, has put it quite candidly:

> Missionary initiative has . . . passed from the hands of Protestants most worried by the ambiguities and moral failures of Western civilization to the conservative evangelicals—the element which is still the most enthusiastic and uncritical purveyor of Western culture to the rest of the world.[14]

My Own Answer—"Yes, But . . ."

As you know, I went twice as a missionary, believing each time that I was being sent out by the Holy Spirit. My sense of call was verified by a denominational sending agency and I am profoundly grateful both to those who sent me and to those who welcomed me. I feel that if I were now in the sunrise of my vocational career rather than headed toward its sunset, I would volunteer again to go. This is my calling.

So my own answer to the question of whether we should send missionaries from the United States to the Third World is also qualified. It is: "Yes, but . . ." I believe we should send them, but I have some ideas about the attitudes we should have and the way we should interpret and implement our missionary task.

For Whose Sake Are We Sending Missionaries?

I think we would do well to pause once in a while and ask ourselves for whose sake we are doing missions. My fellow Baptists and I frequently remember that it was the motive of international missions that brought us together in a national organization in the United States in 1814—though the slavery issue would soon divide us into two denominational bodies. For us, the missionary impulse is a unifying force of great significance. Without a doubt the Southern Baptist Convention "needs" its extensive program of missions, both at home and abroad, to motivate us and especially to counteract the divisive forces which threaten to pull us apart. But are we missionary primarily for the sake of what missions will do for us?

An African Christian, Canon Burgess Carr, formerly general secretary of the All Africa Conference of Churches, in striking language has charged American Christians with doing missions to save our own souls. He tells us that we discovered that by sending missionaries we could fulfill our responsibility—

to spread the Gospel to the ends of the earth and in one stroke become
a Good Samaritan and an Evangelist. Naturally, people leaped at the
offer. What surer way to climb Jacob's ladder to glory? It meant that
a slavemaster in Georgia could save his soul by saving the soul of a
"native" or "heathen" in some faraway jungle.

. . . It was not enough to oppress the "native" politically and exploit
her or him economically. The "native" had also to be the raw material
used to attain your salvation as well. Talk about theological heresy![15]

No doubt, try as we may, we human beings cannot entirely remove
self-interest from our Christian undertakings. But we can carefully
monitor our attitudes to see whether we are devising and operating
our own mission, or whether we are humbly participating in *God's
mission,* for his sake and the gospel's and for the sake of the world.

On This Matter of Attitudes

The attitudes which we bring to our missionary work are of prime
importance. On this subject let me offer a few suggestions.

First of all, I believe that we American Christians must shoulder
our share of the burden of the imperialistic past and present with
humility but without morbidity. There is danger, on the one hand,
that we blithely or naively assume that we are innocent. The British,
Dutch, Germans, French, Spanish, and Portuguese are guilty of past
imperialism; but we are not, we say. Or the Russians are guilty of
neo-imperialism, but we are innocent. A careful study of our history
and our present involvements should free us of such naiveté. We may
be more or less guilty than some other nations, but we are not innocent.

On the other hand, a wrong response to guilt may render us immo-
bile: since we are guilty of political and economic imperialism, past
and present, we shall see to it that no one can charge us with religious
imperialism. So we will oppose missionary activity of American
Christians in Third World countries. This seems to me to be a refusal
of Christian responsibility done in the name of being responsible.
Shouldn't it be rather that because as citizens of the United States we
are not innocent of imperialism, we shall see to it that our missionary
efforts are non-imperialistic? After all, the Christian mission, operating from motives of love and gratitude—"not to be served but to
serve"—is anti-imperialistic. Rather than abandoning our mission we
need to purge it of any lingering imperialistic overtones.

To free missions from imperialism we shall need to learn the facts about American involvement in colonial or neo-colonial activities and do what we can to influence our government to correct those policies. Imperialism is to be opposed because it is a sin against persons, and not only because it is contradictory of Christian missions.

Renouncing imperialism means to renounce the imperialistic set of mind. All attitudes of superiority, whether based on race, culture, religion, or whatever must be expelled from our consciousness. Such attitudes are subtle in their tendency to infiltrate our minds and tenaciously hold their territory there. They may well be demons that come forth only "by prayer and fasting"!

For example, we may easily assume that American "know-how" is superior. Then we feel justified in imposing our ways of doing things upon others. Or, since we are convinced that Jesus Christ is Lord, we feel impelled to see to it that others become Christian. If they refuse, then by that very fact they are sinful or stupid. Such an attitude motivates an imperialistic approach. And it contradicts the mystery of God's love and grace which respects everyone's personhood and freedom and coerces no one.

Also, it is necessary to resist pressures to produce statistical success, the compulsion to be able to report numbers of converts and new congregations. Such pressures may lead to what Kosuke Koyama calls the "crusading mind" as opposed to the "crucified mind." The crusading mind, of course, is the imperialist stance, while the crucified mind is "a mind of self-denial based on Christ's self-denial" and produced by the Crucified One within us.[16]

We most effectively disavow the imperialistic mind-set by affirming the role of servant: "The son of man also came not to be served but to serve, and to give his life . . ." (Mark 10:45). We are to be servants without being servile, slaves without being slavish. The Christ is our great example. Never did he "pull his rank" and lord it over us. Always he was servant of God and of humanity. But never did he compromise his dignity or self-respect. He retained an inner autonomy. The Apostle Paul, following the model of Jesus, was constantly affirming his role as servant: "For what we preach is not ourselves but Jesus Christ as Lord, with ourselves as your servants for Jesus' sake" (2 Corinthians 4:5). Yet with Paul there was no hint of fawning or servility.

The role of servant is also the key to the possibility of the affluent serving the poor. We have already noticed that the American missionary is almost inevitably "wealthy" among the poor of the Third World. Can the affluent follow the pattern of Jesus and "preach the good news to the poor"? It certainly isn't easy! Kosuke Koyama says that often "the well-fed tend to preach to the hungry people that all they need is the word of God." Of course, "the hungry do not recognize sincerity in these words." He concludes that it is very difficult for missionaries sent by a rich and powerful nation to preach the gospel to the poor. "Not impossible," he says, "but difficult."[17] How very difficult!

When my wife and I returned to the States in 1980 after four years in Japan, we began to notice in our society a mood of anger toward the poor. This attitude was illustrated for us in the winter of 1982-1983 when we attended a hearing in our city hall. On the agenda was a proposal to amend the zoning ordinance to permit a church to provide an overnight shelter for the homeless in our city. Many of these homeless were people who were newly unemployed and impoverished by the economic recession. Existing shelters were hopelessly inadequate. I was shocked when a person prominent in city politics spoke against the proposal. She used three terms to refer to these homeless: *winos, drug addicts* and *panhandlers.*

To carry this hostility toward the poor with us into the world of the poor will disqualify us as ministers of Christ among them. Are we not called rather to become one with them, adjusting our life-styles to their poverty and living a life of sharing?

A young woman from Mexico has reminded us that the poor have something we need and can minister to us. She tells how her work in solidarity with the poor of El Salvador transformed her humanistic faith into a fervent Christian faith. She was living a life alienated from the church, seeking to help people, and in that humanistic direction she thought she had found "something sufficient." Then she came really to know poor people, and "the poor, with their suffering, their hope and their faith," she said, "taught me the ways of God. From then on . . . my encounter was not just with 'something' but with 'someone.' With God the Father, the Son who suffers in the suffering flesh of the poor people of El Salvador, the Spirit who moves in us to make all things new."[18]

After all, we do meet the Christ in the faces of "the least of these" who are his brothers and sisters, and whenever we meet the Servant par excellence may we not expect to be ministered to?

Only those who take seriously the role of servant will be able to offset the negative factors which would indicate that American missionaries cannot function effectively in the Third World. Humility was never really an option for the Christian missionary. Today it is an imperative necessity.

Church Selfhood versus Paternalism

But attitudes are not enough. Sensitivity needs to be translated into methods by which we do our missionary work. Our methodology should enhance the selfhood of churches and eliminate paternalism.

But you're probably asking, "Just what is the 'selfhood' of a church?" This question has relevance for all of us who relate to churches and not just for those concerned directly with missionary methodology.

It is not enough to say that selfhood means self-support, self-government, and self-propagation. This "three self" terminology, developed by missionary strategists in the nineteenth century, is useful especially if it is supplemented by a fourth—self-expression. But these three or four "selves" may describe nothing but a selfish or a self-sufficient church and therefore not a Christian church at all.

Nor do I think we are on the right track when we think of church selfhood in terms of some stage of maturity, when the church has produced capable leaders and some measure of financial capability, etc. From the Biblical standpoint, the goal of maturity is always before and beyond the church: it is "the measure of the stature of the fulness of Christ" (Ephesians 4:13) toward which the church is to grow. But at the same time churches are treated as though they have full responsibility for their life and mission from the first. The New Testament seems to assume that as soon as a church comes into being it represents in its own place the body of Christ.[19]

Is not the selfhood of the church, as any other selfhood, discoverable in its essential relationships?[20] As I understand it, a church has four primary relationships: to the Lord God, to the Church universal, to its environing culture and to its own inner life. I suggest, therefore, that a church has Christian selfhood when it is rightly related in faithful obedience to the Lord God revealed in Jesus Christ, who, as indwelling Spirit is the sovereign source of its life and mission;

in cooperation and fellowship with the Church universal, whose reality it manifests locally and whose world mission it shares;

in vital communication with its cultural environment, from which it derives media for interpreting and expressing the universal gospel in its local context; and

in integrity to its own inner life, with a combination of humility and self-respect, ready to "bear its own burden" but also to "bear . . . another's burden" (Galatians 6:1-5).

Seeing the church in this kind of image should certainly discourage paternalistic attitudes.

Now I am ready to suggest some principles of relationship which respect church selfhood and express partnership, not paternalism. I am aware that it is presumptuous for me to construct such principles on my own. Such should be worked out by partners! I can only plead that my suggestions reflect my years of working with Japanese Christians as well as my study of missionary theory. They are subject to correction by thoughtful Christians from the Third World—or from any other world!

Notice also how these principles have to do with money, power, and human dignity. Perhaps the most difficult of these three to deal with is money. Questions of power (authority) and dignity so often center on the use or misuse of money. How many times I have wished we could do missionary work without money! But of course we cannot. How can we American (and other Western) Christians use our greater financial resources without breeding in partner churches overseas a spirit of servility and dependence which violates human dignity and trammels selfhood? How can money be used without its being subtly coercive? How can we avoid the spurious authority which inheres in purse strings?

From a different angle, there is the Saul-David problem. Often, highly organized and institutionalized churches of our culture are cooperating with younger and smaller churches whose life is not so complex and sophisticated. How do we keep from clothing these young Davids in Saul's armor? Or in any case, how do we avoid clothing them in the alien garments of our Western Christianity?

If in situations of human need—for food, medicine, education, and so forth—Christian compassion demands that we develop institutions to minister adequately, do these institutions nurture an unwholesome dependence? Do they inhibit the development of church selfhood?

Some Principles of Partnership

These are difficult questions, certainly without easy answers. Maybe there are no perfect solutions. But at least we can propose some principles for the expression of partnership in international missions.

1. Concerning the number and kinds of missionaries sent to work with existing churches, the judgment of the churches receiving them should be honored. Young churches must not be inundated by too many missionaries. Unless those making personnel decisions are deeply sensitive to the selfhood of the churches, there will not be adequate brakes upon paternalism and imperialism.

2. Financial policies should not be such as to encourage churches to seek money by requesting missionaries. Monetary aid should not be conditioned upon the presence of missionaries.

3. If churches are subsidized, all funds contributed should be placed in the treasury of the churches receiving them, with the expectation that responsible accounting will be made. The dictum "mission money in missionary hands" is not a Christian principle and should be rejected. Responsibility in the use of contributions is a matter of Christian integrity and should be respected.

4. Missionaries should have no authority in the churches receiving them except that assigned to them by those churches. It is assumed that the missionaries will become members of the churches to which they are sent and thus subject to their discipline.

5. The functions of the "mission"—the organization of missionaries in a given nation or area—should be reduced as the churches related to it develop. These churches should help determine what the residual functions of the mission will be, or whether the mission should continue as a separate entity.

6. The adminstration and ownership of "mission" institutions should be placed in the hands of the young churches as soon as possible, which in most cases probably means yesterday! Until this transfer is possible, there should be joint administration.

7. As a rule, there should be systematic reductions of subsidies to churches and institutions. Those responsible for the reductions, both missionaries and national church leaders, will need to be hard-nosed

if continued disbursement of funds nurtures unwholesome dependence and dwarfing of selfhood.

8. Outreach beyond the boundaries of the churches should be magnified. Within reasonable limits, freedom for missionaries to reach the frontiers beyond these borders should be recognized. It is most unfortunate, however, if it is the foreign missionaries alone who serve on the frontiers of the churches to which they are sent, thus suggesting that the mission of the churches is something foreign to them. Happy is the situation where churches cooperate internationally on these frontiers.

9. It follows that true cooperation should be sought, not just a one-way street of missionaries from the West but a multi-directional flow. In recent years the rather rapid development of international missions on the part of Third World churches is quite encouraging and exciting. However, as yet very few of these Third World missionaries are being sent to Western countries.

We in the United States urgently need the witness of Third World Christians. If there is any substance to the charge of the spiritual bankruptcy of the West, then we can profit greatly from the testimony of those who see more clearly than most of us the "congruence between the affluence of Christendom and the sins that Jesus preached against." We should deliberately invite them to "come over and help us"[21]—while being careful, of course, not to encourage a "brain drain" from the Third World.

10. We need to continue the quest for adequate organizational structures of mission which will lift the burden of Western paternalism and enable the churches everywhere to participate as equal partners in mission. The system of missionary boards and societies inherited from the colonial era assigns too much initiative and importance to the Western churches.

Some models of international partnership are already appearing. For example, on a small scale, the United Mission to Nepal has been hailed as an impressive example of cooperation between various denominations of the West and the Third World in missionary efforts. Recently the Southern Baptist Foreign Mission Board added a missionary couple to this team effort. In recent years, also, on a much larger scale, some Western missionary societies have joined together with the churches which have resulted from their missionary work overseas to form international "communities" for world missionary work.[22] In these structures missions are no longer directed from a Western but from an international base. Personnel and finance from Western and Third World churches are shared and international, interracial teams of missionaries are sent. "Only by internationalizing the teams," says Carl Braaten, "can the imperialist, colonialist, or capitalist image of the Christian mission be effaced."[23]

So the new structures for the postcolonial era are gradually appearing. Meantime, American missionary societies will do well to further internationalize themselves by including more Third World Christians on their staffs, and by sending more international, interracial, and interdenominational teams of missionaries.

Undergirding the above suggestions is a particular concept of partnership. In the business world there are unequal partnerships based on controlling interests. One partner may hold a controlling interest in the company by getting possession of 51 percent of the stock. In missionary work, the controlling interest must not be that of the missionary organization and its missionaries but of the young churches. The idea of dominance by the Western mission because of its money ought to be turned on its head. *The controlling interest of missionary work in any country must not be in the hands of foreigners.*

In the "Pioneer" Situations

There are still regions in the world where missionaries truly need to be pioneers, planting churches where there are no existing churches nearby to share responsibility in partnership. In these situations, what should the missionary do to encourage the emergence of churches with authentic Christian selfhood?

I think the missionary as pioneer would do well to seek to communicate a minimal understanding of the Christian faith, help to establish a basic church structure and then commit responsibility to the young churches themselves.

The communication of the meaning of Christian faith would need to be

> *evangelical:* What is the meaning of the gospel?
> *ethical:* How do persons and churches live out the meaning of the confession "Jesus Christ is Lord" in their society?
> *theological:* What, basically, do Christians believe?
> *ecclesiological:* What is the church and how does it function?

This instruction needs to be Biblical, of course—though not oblivious to the history of Christianity and Christian thought—because of the nature of Biblical authority. Also, to focus upon the Bible should help inhibit the missionary from transferring his or her own cultural conditioning and thus aid an indigenous Christianity to develop.

The establishing of a minimum of church structure is necessary so that the church may effectively communicate the gospel, order its life, administer baptism and the Lord's Supper and nurture its members in the faith.

Inevitably, no doubt, the missionary will communicate some measure of his own denominational heritage and convictions. It is to be hoped, however, that he or she will be sensitive to the fact that the church is ecumenical as well as denominational reality. The sensitive missionary, also, will be alert to aspects of the culture which will be relevant to how the church and its message may be expressed. Of utmost importance is the freedom of the young church, upon the basis of the knowledge communicated to it and the immediate presence of the Holy Spirit, to determine and develop its own patterns of church life.

So it behooves the missionary to be willing to commit responsibility to the young church, to trust the Holy Spirit, to take whatever steps are necessary to avoid too dominant a role in its continuing life. One recalls the Pauline pattern:[24] the missionary communicated the gospel, gathered a community of believers, appointed elders and then moved on, keeping up with them by his prayers, letters, and visits. The missionary should know how to distance himself from the churches of his planting, whether the distancing is geographical or psychological, in order not to get in the way of the churches' selfhood.

There are still other pioneer situations where the missionary from outside will not be admitted as evangelist or church planter but only as a specialist who can contribute a needed service to a developing nation. The missionary may be permitted entrance to develop or serve a hospital, clinic or school, for instance, but not to do overt evangelism. In such cases, of course, not all of the principles we have suggested are applicable.

While as a rule institutions should not be developed which the young churches themselves cannot be expected to support, there are circumstances where tragic human need requires institutional expressions of Christian love supported by American churches. Sometimes love can neither turn away nor wait indefinitely when confronted by the poignant cry of need.

All of which is to say that Christian missions must have methods and principles by which selfhood of churches and cooperative partnership are furthered.

Shall we continue to send missionaries from America into the Third World? Yes, by all means! But let us be careful to strengthen rather than impede the development of the selfhood of the churches now existing or yet to be called into being by the Holy Spirit in that vast area. And let us go with attitudes and methods which are consistent with the gospel of grace and the practice of servanthood.

NOTES

1. A. Ginting-Suka, "The Development Issue in Indonesia," IDOC Dossier No. 9, *The Future of the Missionary Enterprise* (1974), p. 117.

2. Jose Miguez-Bonino, "The Present Crisis in Mission," ibid., p. 75. First published in *Church Herald,* Nov. 12, 1971.

3. Emerito Nacpil, "Mission but Not Missionaries," ibid., p. 80. Previously published in *International Review of Mission,* July, 1971.

4. Neville D. Jayaweera, "Christian Communication in the Third World," *The Role of North Americans in the Future of the Foreign Missionary Enterprise,* (Veutnor, N.J.: Overseas Ministries Study Center, 1982) p. 110. Photocopied from *Occasional Essays* (San Jose, Costa Rica), October, 1979.

5. Orlando E. Costas, *Christ Outside the Gate* (Maryknoll, NY: Orbis Books, 1982), p. 34.

6. Ibid., p. 77.

7. Ibid., pp. 73, 118-119.

8. Raul S. Manglapus, "Global Justice and the American Dream," IDOC Dossier No. 17, *The Future of the Missionary Enterprise* (1976), p. 13.

9. John Gatu, "Missionary, Go Home," IDOC Dossier No. 9, pp. 70-74. First published in *Church Herald.*

10. Jayaweera, "Christian Communication in the Third World", p. 112.

11. Gatu, "Missionary, Go Home."

12. David M. Stowe, in *Mission Handbook,* Twelvth Edition, p. 10.

13. Federico Pagura, "Missionary, Go Home . . . or Stay," *Mission Trends No. 1,* ed. by Gerald H. Anderson and Thomas F. Stransky (Paulist Press and Eerdmans Publishing Co., 1974), pp. 115-116. Reprinted from *The Christian Century,* April 11 1973.

14. Wilbert Shenk, "Which Paradigm for Mission?" *Mission Focus: Current Issues,* ed. by Wilbert Shenk (Scottsdale, Penna.: Herald Press, 1980), p. 160.

15. Burgess Carr, "Internationalizing the Mission," IDOC Dossier No. 9, p. 73.

16. Kosuke Koyama, "What Makes a Missionary? Toward Crucified Mind not Crusading Mind," *Mission Trends No 1*, pp. 130-132.

17. Kosuke Koyama, "The Crucified Christ Challenges Human Power," *Your Kingdom Come, Report on the World Conference on Mission and Evangelism, Melbourne, Australia, 12-25 May 1980* (Geneva: WCC, 1980), p. 160.

18. " 'The Poor of El Salvador Brought Me to God'—Interview with Blanca," *International Review of Mission,* LXXII: 287 (July 1983), p. 413.

19. Compare R. Pierce Beaver, *The Missionary between the Times* (Garden City, N.Y.: Doubleday, 1968), p. 128.

20. I have discussed the selfhood of the church more fully in E. Luther Copeland, "Indigenous and More: toward Authentic Selfhood," *Journal of Ecumenical Studies,* 11:3 (Summer 1974), pp. 501-513.

21. See Costas, *Christ Outside the Gate,* pp. 81-83.

22. Three that have formed international communities are the Latin American Mission, the Paris Evangelical Mission Society and the former London Missionary Society.

23. Carl E. Braaten, *The Flaming Center* (Philadelphia: Fortress Press, 1977), p. 88.

24. See Roland Allen, *Missionary Methods: St. Paul's or Ours?* Third edition (London: World Dominion Press, 1933).

7

Can We Achieve a Livable World?
World Mission
and Survival Issues

Not only is the kingdom of God, God's new order, to be represented by the missionary sent to some other culture. It is to be modeled by Christians and churches everywhere. The communication of the good news of God's new order in one's own community and to the ends of the earth must be undergirded and not contradicted by the witness of Christian lives universally. So the Christian world mission requires ethical choices and value judgments consistent with the new order of God's intention.

What is the basic ethical challenge to all people today? I believe it is simply the issue of whether we can *live* for a forseeable future, whether we can *live together,* and whether we can survive in conditions which make life *worth living.*

Our human technology has brought us together in one world with amazing potential for a future but simultaneously with the dread possibilities of universal annihilation or irreparable injury to ourselves and our environment.

The fundamental question, then, is whether we human beings can survive in a livable world. Under this great umbrella issue are some subheadings which I like to call "survival issues." Each one is inseparable to the Christian mission and each must be addressed by the church everywhere—if we are committed to God's kingdom, the new order of his intention.

War and Peace

First, there is the complex of issues related to war and peace. This century has witnessed for the first time in history war on a global scale—the horror of two world wars—and the development of incredible weapons of destruction. Since 1945 we have been unable to escape the shadow of a giant mushroom-shaped cloud.

Hiroshima, Peace Park, Thousand Crane Memorial to children who died in 1945 atomic bomb blast.

The two most powerful nations on earth have the capability of destroying each other and indeed all of human life. Tragically, their official attitudes toward each other, apart from what may be the sentiments of their peoples, are predominantly mutual suspicion and distrust if not outright animosity. Meanwhile, both continue to add to their nuclear arsenals and to refine their capabilities for destruction. And fully as ominously, less powerful nations increasingly join the nuclear death club.

The amount of money spent on the arms race boggles the mind. Since 1979 the rate of annual increases in spending has greatly accelerated. According to the U.S. Arms Control and Disarmament Agency, world military spending is expected to exceed $1 trillion in 1985! The United States and the Soviet Union, with their respective allies, account for nearly 75 percent of the arms sold.[1] To contemplate what it would mean if this amount had been spent to meet massive needs for the basics of life—food, shelter, water supply, health, education, etc.—likewise taxes the imagination.

Clearly, here is an issue of inexpressible importance and urgency. The Christian mission, in a fundamental sense, is a ministry of reconciliation. Christian peacemaking in a post-Hiroshima era must not be left merely to the politicians. Peacemaking is an issue for all persons of goodwill, whether absolute pacifists or not. And how can any of us be other than pacifists with regard to *nuclear* war?

From time to time the Christian conscience finds expression on this survival issue. In November of 1981, the World Council of Churches brought together an international group of distinguished leaders of church and political life for a "Hearing on Nuclear Weapons and Disarmament." Forty expert witnesses testified and several background papers were presented. The result was a report approved by the Central Committee of the WCC in 1982. The detailed report included the following statements:

> We believe that the time has come when the churches must unequivocally declare that the production and deployment as well as the use of nuclear weapons are a crime against humanity and that such activities must be condemned on ethical and theological grounds.
>
> . . .
>
> We realize that this places a special responsibility on Christians in those countries which possess nuclear weapons and especially on

churches in the two major powers, the USA and the USSR. These countries and their allies bear a heavy burden of responsibility for the nuclear arms race and nuclear weapons proliferation.[2]

Subsequently, in May, 1983, the United States bishops of the Catholic Church, after a lengthy process attended by considerable controversy, approved a Pastoral Letter on War and Peace entitled *The Challenge of Peace: God's Promise and Our Response.* Let me include but one eloquent excerpt from this comprehensive document:

> The whole world must summon the moral courage and technical means to say no to nuclear conflict; no to weapons of mass destruction; no to an arms race which robs the poor and the vulnerable; and no to the moral danger of a nuclear age which places before humankind indefensible choices of constant terror or surrender. Peacemaking is not an optional commitment. It is a requirement of faith. We are called to be peacemakers, not by some movement of the moment, but by our Lord Jesus.[3]

These are prominent examples of public statements deriving from the deep urgings of the prophetic conscience and directed to the powerful. No less commendable are the quiet efforts of peacemakers who take the time to study the issue of peace in a nuclear age and give their witness less dramatically. An example is the Baptist Peacemaker group at Deer Park Baptist Church, Louisville, Kentucky, who publish *Baptist Peacemaker,* a remarkably well-informed periodical.

Is it not time for all churches to put peacemaking as a separate and priority item on their agendas? Some are doing so. Cannot we come up with something new and creative on this matter?

A proposal for a United States Academy of Peace is now before the Congress. It would have functions of research, teaching and information sharing. Students could take graduate or post-graduate courses or mid-career seminars and workshops. This proposal has a long history. It derives from recommendations for a national department of peace dating back to 1793. It was sanctioned by the Bishops' Pastoral Letter mentioned previously. Surely here is an idea whose time has at last come. Another idea of merit is a proposed International Task Force for Peacemaking and Conflict Resolution to be established by the United Nations.

Poverty and Hunger

Inseparable from the question of war and peace is a second survival issue, that of poverty and hunger—actually a cluster of problems having to do with poverty. For millions of human beings the threat of nuclear annihilation takes a back seat to the constant specter of death because of hunger or hunger-related causes. Closely related are problems of inadequate housing, illiteracy, disease, conflict, and crime.

The number of people living in absolute poverty, "a state of . . . silent genocide," is constantly increasing. They now number 890 million, about one fifth of the human race! About 500 million are on the edge of starvation. Over 800 million adults are illiterate and their number is still rising. Some 120 million young people of school age have no school to attend. An estimated 600 million people are unemployed or underemployed.[4] The number of permanently unsettled refugees is ten million or more. Some estimates say sixteen million.[5]

American Christians are carrying on large programs of world relief and development through various agencies such as Church World Service of the Division of Overseas Ministries of the National Council of Churches, World Relief Corporation of the National Association of Evangelicals, World Vision, American Friends Service Committee, the Baptist World Alliance, the Foreign Mission Board of the Southern Baptist Convention, Lutheran World Relief, and the United Methodist Committee on Relief. These are the largest organizations among some 150 in North America. Most of them administer not only programs of emergency relief but also various self-help programs seeking to enable the poor to support themselves. In many instances, missionaries are the personnel who operate the programs.

How to deal with world poverty is a complex problem indeed. It is encouraging to note that Christians, including conservative evangelicals, are grappling with this complicated issue and seeking its root causes. A good example is one of the volumes prepared for the Wheaton '83 Conference under the title *The Church in Response to Human Need*.[6] Also, one of the *Lausanne Occasional Papers* deals with "Christian Witness to the Urban Poor." It is an impressive document.

While the gospel of Christ is good news for all people, it is specifically designated as "good news to the poor" (Luke 4:18; compare Matt. 11:5). The Bible never speaks disparagingly of the poor. Rather,

God is invariably represented as their champion. The good news to the poor is that God is on their side because he is the God of justice. And the good news must surely include the disclosure that God's people are also on the side of the poor, not sharing the world's hostility or indifference toward them, and are prepared to help get at the causes of their poverty so that they, their children, and their children's children, may be assured of a future and thus may live in hope.

The poor of all societies must be a priority concern of the Christian mission. The fact that most of the poor and the poorest of the poor are in the Third World is another reason we cannot escape our missionary responsibility for that vast area.

Justice and Human Rights

It is an understatement to say that the dimensions of injustice in the world today are of shocking proportions. There are many oppressive regimes, of both rightist and leftist ideologies. Thousands of persons have been executed under the fundamentalist Islamic regime in Iran including pregnant women and children under sixteen. Baha'is are suffering terrible persecution in that tortured land. Soviet dissenters are held in mental institutions and "treated" with powerful drugs. Thousands of defenseless people have been slaughtered in Central America. And here in America, child abuse is tragically prevalent.[7] These are but examples of a shockingly widespread phenomenon of oppression, cruelty, torture, violence, and death.

In democracies there is hope that the denial of basic human rights can be corrected by the peaceful processes of legislation and judicial procedures. Even so, at times demonstrations and civil disobedience are deemed necessary to protest unjust laws or discriminatory policies and achieve justice. In tyrannical societies there is the ruthless suppression of dissent and protest. Violent revolution often results.

In some parts of the world liberation movements seek overthrow of oppressive regimes. In Latin America, particularly, a theology of liberation has emerged in the last twenty years in the production and furtherance of which many Roman Catholics and a lesser number of Protestants are involved.

Of course, the issue we are discussing is much broader than liberation movements. There are many situations in which basic human rights are being denied and persons are suffering oppression without any definite movement in process to seek their relief. American foreign policy is involved, also, when it is perceived that the United States is supporting an oppressive regime for alleged reasons of national self-interest. Or there may be cases, as we have noted, in which the United States is viewed by people of a Third World country as an oppressor. In such situations, ethical judgments are required by all citizens of our democracy and not just missionaries and missionary administrators.

The issue of whether or how missionaries from the United States should identify with those who are oppressed puts the missionary in a peculiarly difficult position. Ordinarily, to work for liberation means to engage in what is interpreted as political activity. But missionaries, as noncitizens of the countries to which they are sent, not only may be subject to expulsion for political involvements, but their actions may also imperil the continued presence of other missionaries. Of course, in the deeper sense, the missionary along with all of us is not merely a citizen of his own country but also a citizen of the world and a member of the whole human family.

Ted Ward, an American educator deeply involved in Third World development and a shrewd observer and interpreter of international missions, has stated that missionaries cannot be "apolitical" in a world "where every human act has a political meaning." He predicts that missionary agencies will become further polarized over political conflicts:

> Some will persist in asserting their nonpolitical nature and will thus continue to aid the status quo, for good or for evil. Others will accept their political meaning and influence. They will be swept up in ever more complex webs of intrigue and decision-making about matters they would far rather leave alone. There are no easy choices; one wonders if, after all, the naive may inherit the world of foreign missions. If so, the era will soon close.[8]

Indeed, "there are no easy choices"! About two years ago, a committee of the Division of Overseas Ministries of the National Council of Churches drew up a statement suggesting guidelines for missionary involvement in issues of justice and human rights.[9] The statement has realism because it relies heavily upon the experiences of missionaries and local churches. Yet, inevitably, much must be left up to the consciences and informed judgments of individual missionaries and missionary agencies drawing upon whatever resources of collective wisdom they can muster.

Perhaps most missionary agencies attempt to maintain sensitivity to human need and to opportunities to help those who suffer on the one hand and a policy of nonpolitical involvement on the other. Such is the policy of the Southern Baptist Foreign Mission Board under which I served as a missionary. Probably this is the best mission boards can do in such complicated circumstances. Certainly, *partisan* politics may be avoided. Nevertheless, political neutrality in the strict sense is impossible in a world where, as Ted Ward says, "every act has a political meaning." Press releases and various publications of mission agencies will inevitably reflect political convictions, for example, a preference for democracy over communism. To discuss liberation theology at all will communicate political nuances. I was aware in Japan that just to be an American had various political meanings for the Japanese.

Let me venture a few personal observations about this most difficult and basically insoluble problem, particularly from the standpoint of the missionary, but not presuming to try to speak for all.

1. Missionaries, in trying to conform to the policy of their sending agency and at the same time keep faith with their consciences, will interpret their responsibilities and determine their behavior differently.[10] Agencies do well to permit their missionaries some flexibility on such an excruciatingly difficult issue.

2. Missionaries from the United States need to take care lest they be co-opted or exploited by political forces in their situation abroad, or by American foreign policy, whether explicitly by the CIA or more subtly by the inner compulsion to communicate and defend American policy. The missionary is an ambassador of Christ and not an envoy of Washington, D.C., or any other political entity.

3. Missionaries need to be knowledgeable politically concerning their own country and the countries to which they are sent. The best way to prevent oneself from being used politically is to know the political realities of one's situation.

4. Obviously where there is oppression, the Christian's place is with the oppressed and not with the oppressors. How missionaries express and implement this identity will vary, but the principle must be maintained.

5. It is most reprehensible to sanction a regime because it allows missionary freedom while at the same time it oppresses its own people. The privilege of missionary entrance and residence can be purchased too dearly.

6. As a citizen of the United States the missionary has a unique opportunity, especially while on furlough, to contribute a world perspective to the continual process by which the American public educates itself on world affairs.

7. One's attitude toward revolution should be even-handed. As a Christian, I find it difficult to sanction any revolution which perpetrates violence. However, it certainly seems inconsistent to approve and celebrate the American Revolution of two centuries ago while condemning a modern revolution, similarly violent, in which those rebelling have far greater injustices to protest than did the American colonists.

We live in a dangerous and volatile world where seething resentments at oppression and injury may ignite a world conflagration. Seeking God's kingdom and his justice is a hazardous undertaking, but it is mandatory.

The Priestly Care of the Environment

Another issue which relates to survival is the care of our environment. Gradually we are coming to understand that the maintenance of our world environment is essential to our own survival. We are bound together in the common bundle of life, not only with our fellow human beings but also with the whole of the created order, with this vast world of plants and animals and tiny microscopic organisms and inanimate matter.

A new orientation to our world is necessary. Too long we of the Western world have misunderstood the biblical injunction to "fill the earth and subdue it; and have dominion over" the creatures of the earth (Gen. 1:28). We have sanctioned a radical exploitation of the natural world, both animate and inanimate. Uncontrolled greed combines with advanced technology to threaten the earth with irreversible pollution and wanton destruction.

We too easily forget that human dominion over the earth is to be exercised under God's sovereignty. It is because "The Lord reigns!" that all of nature can rejoice and "sing for joy" (Ps. 96:10-13). The apostle declares that "the creation waits with eager longing for the revealing of the sons of God" (Rom. 8:19). Surely part of his meaning must be that the creation can never hope to be other than exploited and abused until God's children appear upon the scene to represent God's interests in relation to the creation which he pronounced good.

Taken as a whole, the Bible does not suggest that the creation exists only for the sake of human beings. There is evidence that the world existed for millions of years before any of us arrived on the scene. The "creatures great and small" rejoiced in the creation, and the Creator found delight in it for aeons without our presence. Presumably, the creation exists for its own sake and for God's sake as well as ours. It behooves us to be humble and reverent in our care of the world which God has created.

I believe that we human beings are called to be God's priests in relation to the natural world. This meaning may well be included in God's designation of Israel as a "kingdom of priests" (Ex. 19:6), a title which the church inherited (1 Pet. 2:9). The context is God's possession of "all the earth" as well as "all peoples": "You shall be my own possession among all peoples; for all the earth is mine, and you shall be to me a kingdom of priests and a holy nation" (Ex. 19:5-6). We are stewards, but we are more than stewards. The connotation of stewardship may be too mechanical and managerial to express our role adequately. We are priests who view the world with reverence because it is God's handiwork. We are to represent the creation to God and act toward it according to his attitude and intent.

The Gospels and Epistles sometimes use the term *the whole creation* in relation to the good news of redemption. In the missionary commission in the later addition to Mark's Gospel, the good news is to be preached "to the whole creation" (Mark 16:15). In Colossians, Paul declares that the gospel has been "preached to every creature under heaven" (Col. 1:23) while in Romans he sees "the whole creation" groaning in travail together with us as we wait for redemption (Rom. 8:22). (Though translated differently, the same Greek words are used in all these passages.) This redemption involves a "new creation" into which by virtue of our relation to Christ we have already entered (2 Cor. 5:17; Gal. 6:15). Or it means a "whole universe" brought back to God through the redeeming work of Christ (Col. 1:20, GNB. Compare Eph. 1:10).

So we are bound together with the creation in the mutuality of our interdependent existence and in the common hope of our redemption.

Unfortunately, most missionaries have not usually had a concern for "earthkeeping," as some have begun to term this aspect of missionary vocation.[11] William Carey (1761-1834) was an exception. The time he spent on botany and horticulture in India was not merely the pursuit of a fascinating hobby but an integral part of his holistic approach to missions. Thus he promoted the conservation of forests as well as the introduction of new species of plants. He made the first plea for forestation in India, and his garden (or park) in Serampore provided a model for it.[12] No doubt many missionaries, like Carey, especially agriculturists, have been actively engaged in protecting the environment. Most, however, like other Westerners, have been indifferent to environmental issues.

Earthkeeping now should be seen as an essential part of the Christian mission. There is a call for Christians who will give themselves specifically to this vocation and for some to fulfill this calling as cross-cultural missionaries. The larger summons is for all of us to support this aspect of the Christian mission and to contribute to it according to our abilities. This too is a survival issue.

Interreligious Relationships

How do we relate to each other across religious lines? This question, also, may well be a matter of survival. Witness the tragic conflicts involving religion in the Middle East today or in Ireland. Historically, some of the bitterest wars have been motivated by interreligious rivalries and religious imperialisms. In our uncertain and inflammatory age even small interreligious wars may ignite nuclear war with its incalculable devastation.

Christian Unity and Cooperation

An important part of the question is how we relate to each other as Christians. The task of world Christians is far too large for any one body of Christians. For this reason alone cooperation is imperative. More basically, however, cooperation is mandated by the very nature of the church as one: "There is one body and one Spirit, just as you were called to the one hope that belongs to your call, one Lord, one faith, one baptism, one God and Father of us all" (Eph. 4:4-6). Moreover, the mission of God's people is directly related to their unity, as indicated by the words of the "high priestly prayer" of Jesus "that they may all be one; . . . so that the world may believe that thou hast sent me" (John 17:21).

Christians differ on ways to express Christian unity and to cooperate. Unfortunately, some individuals and groups seem unable or unwilling to relate to other Christians at all except to criticize and condemn. Among those who desire to cooperate, the modern ecumenical movement offers a variety of ideals, methodologies, and structures.

The word *ecumenical* derives from a Greek term meaning "the inhabited earth" and refers (1) to Christianity as a community with a universal mission and (2) as a universal household or family of God. Therefore it involves both mission and unity.

The ecumenical movement includes the various attempts to bring Christians together in an expression of their unity in mission. Unfortunately, sometimes mission tends to be lost from sight in the commendable eagerness to get together. These efforts at unity range all the way from church unions such as the Church of South India, formed in 1947 from several denominations—including Anglicans and nonepiscopal churches in union for the first time in history—to interor nondenominational agencies for cooperation of individual Christians, such as the YMCA and YWCA.

The largest stream of ecumenical cooperation is that of "conciliar" structures, that is, councils of churches and Christian councils, local, national, regional, and international in which churches cooperate while retaining their denominational identities. The largest are the World Council of Churches (WCC) and the National Council of Churches of Christ in the U.S.A. (NCC). The conciliar movement has minimal confessional requirements. However, the "Basis" of the WCC and the "Preamble" to the Constitution of the NCC tend to exclude churches with unitarian theologies. Most of the major Protestant denominations belong to these councils along with Orthodox churches. Cordial relations are maintained with the Roman Catholic Church.

Conservative evangelicals have formed their own ecumenical structures, largely in reaction to the conciliar movement. They criticized the latter as too liberal, lacking a creedal affirmation of the infallibility of the Bible, and espousing the "social gospel." So far as the United States is concerned, the most important of the conservative evangelical organizations are the National Association of Evangelicals (NAE) and the World Evangelical Fellowship (WEF) of which the former is a member. A narrower and more stridently fundamentalist kind of

(Left to right) Hugo Culpepper, E. Luther Copeland, Muhammad Abdul Rauf, participants in Baptist-Muslim dialogue, Toledo, Ohio, 1972.

ecumenism is represented by the American Council of Christian Churches (ACCC) and the International Council of Christian Churches (ICCC) associated with the initiative and leadership of Carl McIntire. Generally, subscription to a conservative confessional statement is required for membership in the conservative evangelical organizations.

In general, the gap between conciliar ecumenism and that of conservative evangelicals has tended to close somewhat in recent years as the former becomes more concerned with evangelism and the latter with social action. Nevertheless, the WCC and NCC continue to be criticized for alleged support of leftist liberation movements.

In the actual operation of missions, the denominations which have emerged in Western history have been transplanted overseas, though in some instances missionaries tried to prevent this from happening. It is true, also, that conflicts between denominations, and especially between so-called liberal and conservative Christians, sometimes have been exported and bequeathed to the young churches with deplorable results.

On the other hand, comity has often been practiced in determining places of work so as to prevent overlapping and unseemly rivalry. More often than not, comity has worked well on an informal basis. An encouragement toward interdenominational cooperation for missionaries and young churches is the fact that they often view themselves as Christian minorities facing gigantic tasks of evangelization, sometimes in a hostile environment. In the face of this reality, denominational differences have not seemed so important.

It has been common, also, for Christians of the non-Western world to view the denominational divisions of the West as something outside their own history and responsibility, "divisions for which we were not responsible, and which have been, as it were, imposed upon us from without," as a group of Indian Christian leaders put it.[13] It is not surprising, therefore, that some of the young churches, products of Western missions, have achieved some interdenominational mergers which are much more difficult to arrive at in the West. At the same time, they have developed some new varieties of Christianity as well, especially in Africa, where there has been a burgeoning growth of independent church movements led by charismatic African leaders.

Christian mission and Christian unity are inseparable. While there is room for differing convictions about ways of achieving, enhancing, and maintaining Christian cooperation and unity, there can be no doubt about their imperative necessity. "If you have love for one another," says the Lord, "then everyone will know that you are my disciples" (John 13:35, GNB). Universally, Christians are called to model the life of the family of God in the new order. If we fight and destroy each other, then we ourselves become a threat to survival in a livable world.

Relating to Persons of Other Religions

In the vast complexity of religions which elicit the commitments of people today, what is the Christian stance? The Christian approach? Christians are diverse individuals standing within different traditions. It would be unrealistic and unreasonable to expect all to share some uniform position. Perhaps, however, we can suggest a framework within which individual choices may be made for a Christian approach to persons of other faiths.

1. *Witness.* Christians are instructed to be witnesses—perhaps it is more accurate to say that they are declared or designated witnesses by the risen Christ. After recounting what had happened to him in the light of the Scriptures, the risen Lord told his disciples, "You are witnesses of these things" (Luke 24:48). Elsewhere he is quoted as saying, "You shall be my witnesses . . . to the end of the earth" (Acts 1:8). (Both phrases seem to be from the "Servant" portions of Isaiah; 43:10, 12; 44:8; 48:20; and 49:6.) Similarly, in the apostolic teaching, Christians are exhorted to be ready, in the face of questioning, contradiction, persecution, "to answer anyone who asks you to explain the hope you have in you, but do it with gentleness and respect" (1 Pet. 3:15-16, GNB).

The first responsibility, then, is for the Christian to know his own faith and be prepared to give a personal testimony concerning it. Witness by its very nature is noncoercive. It depends upon the convincing power of the truth, and in the case of Christian witness, upon the mysterious working of the Holy Spirit. Any coercion or manipulation, psychological or otherwise, is entirely incompatible with Christian evangelism. To coerce or manipulate others in the name of Christian witness is to treat them as objects rather than persons. Not only so, it also manifests a distrust in the convincing power of the truth as applied by the Holy Spirit.

2. *Respect.* The constraints of Christian love require us to have

profound respect for other persons, no matter how mistaken or absurd their beliefs may appear to be. "Be ready . . . to answer, . . . but do it with gentleness and respect." This instruction may be difficult to follow, especially in one's contacts with some bizarre religious groups which seem to turn human beings into robots. Nevertheless, in these cases also, respect for persons is imperative. "Gentleness and respect" are not incompatible with courage and candor.

I have always remembered the word of a great Anglican missionary statesman, the late Max Warren:

> Our first task in approaching another people, another culture, another religion, is to take off our shoes, for the place we are approaching is holy. Else we may find ourselves treading on men's dreams. More serious still, we may forget that God was here before our arrival.[14]

3. *Fairness.* "Treat others as you would like them to treat you" (Luke 6:31, NEB). The Golden Rule requires scrupulous fairness in our estimate of other religions. If it is wrong for a person who is not a Christian to give a consciously biased description of Christian faith, then it is certainly wrong for a Christian to give a distorted interpretation of another's religion. There is a strong temptation to compare our religion at its best with another person's at its worst. This temptation to palpable unfairness must be resisted.

In working among adherents of Buddhism and Shinto, I have never found it necessary or appropriate to speak disparagingly of these religions. If I had done so, I am sure I would have been less effective as a missionary.

4. *Understanding.* The great apostle claimed that he had become all things to all kinds of people that he might "by all means save some" (1 Cor. 9:22). This principle, based upon the incarnation of Christ, means that the Christian seeks to enter into the world of another with love and understanding. Obviously, not all of us can achieve genuine understanding of all religions—perhaps none of us. But certainly it is essential for missionaries at least to become knowledgeable about the religion of the area where they are working.

Though one may feel that his understanding of another religion is never adequate, it is the attitude of vital interest, the will to understanding and empathy, which is imperative for witnesses of Christ in a pluralistic world. The late Hendrik Kraemer, with permissible exaggeration, stated that the only point of contact between the gospel and its hearers who were not Christians

> *is the missionary worker himself.* Such is the golden rule . . . in this whole matter. The way to live up to this rule is to have an untiring and genuine interest in the religion, the ideas, the sentiments, the institutions—in short, in the whole range of life of the people among whom one works, *for Christ's sake and for the sake of those people.*
> . . . As long as a man feels that he is the object of interest only for reasons of intellectual curiosity or for purposes of conversion, and not because of himself as he is in his total empirical reality, there cannot arise that humane natural contact which is the indispensable condition of all real religious meeting of man with man.[15]

5. *The Practice of Dialogue.* In recent years, planned conversations involving adherents of different religions have become fairly common. For the most part this interreligious dialogue has been initiated by Christians in an effort at mutual understanding. However, many Christians have been distrustful and fearful of dialogue as involving some compromise of Christian faith or as becoming a substitute for evangelism. Some persons of other religions, on the other hand, have looked askance at dialogue as a possible disguise for Christian attempts to convert them.

By now, however, interreligious dialogue has to some extent dispelled these fears and established itself as a means to build bridges of understanding. My own experience of dialogue has given me a better understanding of my own faith as well as the faith of others. It has also given me firmer underpinnings for Christian evangelism. While the Christian enters into dialogue with persons of other religions with the sincere purpose of deeper understanding, the more fundamental purpose of his or her life cannot be set aside, namely, to be a faithful witness of Jesus Christ.[16]

Apart from formal dialogue, however, the dialogical relationship is of basic importance for Christian evangelism. One needs to listen as well as speak and to listen *before* speaking. This is another way of stating the incarnational principle, that the missionary needs to enter into the world of other persons. C. F. Andrews, a renowned Anglican missionary, was once asked, "How do you preach the gospel to a Hindu?" Andrews replied, "I don't. I preach the gospel to a man."

D. T. Niles, in reporting this incident, stresses the fact that the gospel is always addressed to a person.[17]

However, I believe it was Niles who somewhere else indicated that we need to know who this person is to whom we are addressing the gospel. He illustrated by saying that to witness to someone without knowing who he is—whether Hindu, Buddhist, etc.—is like trying to step from the platform onto a moving train as it leaves the station. This approach, said Niles, could be disastrous! Rather, one must approximate the speed of the train and then step on.

One needs to listen before speaking. This is similar to John A. Mackay's admonition that the Christian needs to win "the right to be heard." "This right is won," said Mackay, "when non-Christians, or merely nominal Christians, are eager to know what Christians have to *say* because they have learned to respect them for what they *are.*"[18] Only by caring deeply about the other and entering into his world do we earn the right to be heard.

6. *A Theological Perspective.* Finally, it is of vital importance that the Christian approach persons of other faiths with a theological perspective regarding the plurality of religions. What is the meaning of this diversity? Are the various religions products of demonic deception foisted upon human beings? Are they simply human systems containing both truth and error? Are they at least partially produced by God's revealing activity, but distorted and incomplete, to be corrected and fulfilled by the revelation in Christ? Or, are some of them demonic deceptions while others are more closely related to God's revealing activity? Or, again, are they something more complex than these questions imply?

On the theological meaning of religious diversity, Christians take differing viewpoints. I suggested earlier that uniformity is neither expected nor desired. What is to be hoped is that Christians will hold the conviction of the universal relevance and urgency of the good news of Jesus Christ in hearts that love, respect, and sympathize with all persons in their religion or lack of it.

God has done something unique and wonderful in Jesus Christ for the salvation of all persons and of the entire creation. In humility and reverence the Christian seeks to share this good news with everybody. And this gospel of God's free but costly grace addresses itself to all persons, religious or irreligious, with the imperative invitation to receive the Lord and Savior who purposes to redeem all of life and make all things new.

When I was in India for a year to do research on Indian religions, my family and I lived on the campus of a large Hindu university to which I was attached. December came, and I was asked to give some lectures on comparative religion, attended by teachers and graduate students of two departments of the university. By that time I had been on the campus for about four months but I felt that I was still held very much at arm's length by the Hindu teachers.

In a discussion period after one of my lectures, a Hindu professor put me on the spot. She cited the case of an American philosopher whom I knew only by some of his writings. Having grown up as a Christian, this scholar had become a Buddhist. "Now, do you think it was beneficial for Professor So-and-So to convert to Buddhism?" asked the Hindu professor.

I replied that I knew little about Professor So-and-So but that so far as I was concerned he had a right to choose whatever religion he wished.

Then she said, "Let's not make the question specific. In general, do you believe it is beneficial for people to convert from their ancestral religion to another?"

Of course, I knew what was behind her question: the Hindu antipathy toward Muslim and Christian attempts to convert Hindus. I asked her, "Do you want me to respond as a student of comparative religion or as a person of religious faith?"

"As you please," she replied.

So I said, "I think I have answered in my lectures from the standpoint of comparative religion, stressing the necessity of freedom in the quest for truth. Some of you, no doubt, would think I would be greatly benefited if I were to accept your deepest religious convictions. As a Christian, I would merely say that Jesus Christ is everything to me, and I would be delighted if everyone in this room shared with me the conviction that he is Lord and Savior."

She had no more questions and, interestingly, from that moment I had rapport with faculty members, including the professor who had interrogated me. Some sought me out to talk about religion, and I had opportunities in these conversations to tell of the hope I have in Christ, "with gentleness and respect." I felt that somehow I had won "the right to be heard."

Religious freedom is immeasurably precious. Christians need to respect and promote it fully for all persons. And we need to work faithfully for peaceful and fraternal relations among people of various convictions. This is right and Christian. It is also one important means of seeking to insure survival in a pluralistic world.

Notes

1. *Light* (Nashville: Christian Life Commission, SBC), July, 1984, p. 10.

2. Paul Abrecht and Ninan Koshy, ed., *Before It's Too Late* (Geneva: WCC, 1983), pp. 32-33.

3. *Origins: NC Documentary Service,* 13, No. 1 (May 19, 1983), p. 30.

4. Ruth Leger Siward, *World Military and Social Expenditures, 1983* (Washington, D.C.: World Priorities, 1983), p. 26.

5. Edward R. Dayton and Samuel Wilson eds., *Unreached Peoples '83,* (Monrovia, Calif.: MARC, 1983) p. 177. This source prefers the lower figure.

6. Tom Sine, ed., *The Church in Response to Human Need* (Monrovia, Calif.: MARC, 1983), especially pp. 22-95.

7. Amnesty International communications of Apr. 15 and Sept. 22 1983.

8. Ted Ward, "Christian Missions—Survival in What Forms?" *International Bulletin of Missionary Research,* 6, No. 1 (Jan. 1982), p. 2.

9. "The Development of Guidelines on Missionary Involvement in Social-Justice and Human-Rights Issues," ibid., pp. 9-12.

10. For examples of missionaries of the same board taking different stances in the same situation, see Martha Skelton, "Conscience in Context," *The Commission,* 46, No. 2 (Feb.-Mar. 1983), pp. 49-53. Several articles in this issue treat the problem of "politics and missions."

11. Dennis E. Testerman, *Missionary Earthkeeping—For God So Loved Africa.* Unpublished paper, Southeastern Baptist Theological Seminary, 1983. In the following discussion, I am indebted to Testerman, especially for some bibliographical leads.

12. Ibid., p. 20. See especially S. Pearce Carey, *William Carey* (New York: George H. Doran Company, 1923), pp. 159, 389-399.

13. Cited in Ruth Rouse and Stephen Charles Neill, eds., *A History of the Ecumenical Movement, 1514-1948* (Philadelphia: Westminister Press, 1954), p. 473.

14. M. A. C. Warren, "General Introduction," *Christian Presence Series.* See George Appleton, *On the Eightfold Path* (New York: Oxford University Press, 1961), p. 10.

15. Hendrik Kraemer, *The Christian Message in a Non-Christian World* (New York: Harper and Brothers, 1938), p. 140.

16. See Lesslie Newbigin, *The Open Secret* (Grand Rapids: Wm. B. Eerdmans Publishing Company, 1978), pp. 205-206.

17. D. T. Niles, *Upon the Earth* (New York: McGraw-Hill Book Company, 1962), p. 235.

18. John A. Mackay, *Ecumenics, The Science of the Church Universal* (Englewood Cliffs, NJ: Prentice-Hall, 1964), pp. 178-186.

8
"Forward Through the Ages . . .
Bound by God's Far Purpose"[1]

I once heard Dr. Elmer West, a staff member of the Southern Baptist Foreign Mission Board, preach a sermon on this theme entitled, "Bound by God's Far Purpose." These words from a Christian hymn convey the picture of God's people pressing on through history on mission bound by a purpose which is as ancient as eternity and as far or as near as the end of history. They suggest a kind of joyous urgency. The Christian mission is joyous: it is a sharing of "good news of a great joy" (Luke 2:10). And it is urgent: the good news is a matter of life and death.

At times our urgent mission may seem more burdensome than joyous. Often the gospel is not perceived as good news at all, and it meets with resentment and resistance. This book has suggested more than once that American Christians are not always viewed as bearers of good news in the Third World.

However, here is an illustration, not from the Third World but from our own society. Several years ago, in a Jewish-Christian dialogue session, as a member of a panel I had felt it necessary to confess my conviction that Christians have an obligation to share the good news of Jesus the Messiah with Jews as well as all other people. Whereupon a Jewish scholar, in some agitation, stood up, pointed his finger at me, and said, "Dr. Copeland, you are a bigot! You think that what you believe is superior to what other people believe."

Other Jewish participants joined him in trying to make us Christians understand what a burden it is for Jews to be objects of Christian evangelism. Somewhat nettled by the charge leveled against me, I tried to convey something of the burden of being a bearer of the gospel, the burden of being viewed as a bigot!

(By the way, my hurt feelings were somewhat assuaged by what followed. A rabbi came to my defense, saying, "Copeland is right, you

133

know. As a Christian, he has to keep inviting us Jews to become Christians. And as a Jew, I have to keep saying no!" I later chatted with the professor who had called me a bigot. In our conversation, he admitted that he too had some beliefs which he considered better than the beliefs of some others, and therefore, said he, "I also am a bigot." I told him it wasn't quite so bad to be a bigot if he and I could be bigots together!)

I profited greatly from that rather painful encounter. I learned in a new dimension the necessity of understanding those who view the Christian mission as imperiling their very existence. This Jewish friend who called me a bigot saw the Christian mission as threatening Jews with genocide. He used that very word. To his understanding, the Christian message was by no means good news! Isn't his anxiety understandable in a post-Hitler, post-Holocaust era? Must we not be able to assure our Jewish friends that they can become Christians without becoming Gentiles—just as the early church had to decide that Gentiles could become Christians without becoming Jews?

What Right Do We Have
to Be Missionary?

What right do we have to this kind of effrontery: to go about sharing "good news" at which many people take umbrage? It may help a bit to remember that there is nothing all that new about this situation. In the first century, the message of the crucified Christ was "offensive to the Jews and nonsense to the Gentiles" (1 Cor. 1:23, GNB). While we certainly must remove any unnecessary offenses from our communication of the gospel, the fact is that it is still offensive to many Jews, Muslims, Hindus, Buddhists, and others, and nonsense to many sophisticated secularists.

What right do we have to be missionary? Let me clarify this question. I do not mean simply what right do Christians have to go somewhere as missionaries. I am asking, by what authority is the church constrained to communicate the meaning of Jesus Christ to the world?

I believe that the authority for this most audacious mission must be the ultimate authority, or else it will not sustain us. We will not move "forward through the ages"—not through our ominous age— without some assurance of ultimate validity. Therefore, we must press the question of our right to mission as far as it will go.

Is it enough to say, as many do, that the Great Commission is the only authority we need? The Great Commission, in its several versions in the four Gospels and Acts, (Matt. 28:19-20; Mark 16:15-18; Luke 24:45-49; Acts 1:8; John 21:21-23) is a powerful impetus to thrust us "forward through the ages," to the ends of the earth and the end of the age. But a mere command cannot be an *ultimate* authority. The command itself is a secondary authority, depending upon the authority of the one commanding.

The understanding of the Great Commission as a command or law can make the Christian mission a legalistic enterprise which produces a legalistic Christianity. Besides, taken as a whole, the commissions were more in the nature of a statement of fact than an imperative, more promise than command.[2] When Paul explained his ministry as "apostle [missionary] to the Gentiles," as he frequently did (Acts 20:24; 22:6-16; Galatians 1: 11-17; 1 Corinthians 15:8-11), it was not on the basis of an earlier commission given to the apostles but a similar commission given to him personally in his encounter with the risen Christ.

The foundation for mission, therefore, lies not so much in some external command or law as in our encounter with the One who is the supreme authority.

What about the Bible as the authority for mission? The Bible is the authoritative, indispensable witness to the living God who has revealed himself in the history of his people Israel and supremely in Jesus of Nazareth. But the Bible always points beyond itself to the God who inspired and validates it:

> Beyond the sacred page
> I seek thee, Lord;
> My spirit pants for thee,
> O living Word.[3]

Or there may be those who think of authority for mission primarily in terms of an inner conviction. But from where does this conviction derive? Surely not from oneself. Not only individual Christians but the church collectively is called to mission. And the authority for this bold task must be more than a subjective matter. Missionary conviction is certainly necessary, but if it does not derive from the living God, then it is inadequate to validate our persistent thrust "forward through the ages."

Sometimes, sensitive to the tragic fact of human need, we may be inclined to think that this desperate human situation itself is all the authority required for our mission as Christians. Certainly the clamant need of the world gives direction to mission and accentuates its urgency. But there is something even deeper.

Imagine, if you can, a situation where the poignant needs which evoke our ministries are all satisfied. We have come to the final city where God himself has wiped away all tears. Death, grief, crying, and pain are gone (Rev. 21:3-4). All are forgiven. All are redeemed. There is abounding joy. What would we do? If we believe what we testify in song, the basic foundation for mission would not have disappeared though its goal may have been attained.

> When this poor lisping, stammering tongue
>   Lies silent in the grave,
> Then in a nobler, sweeter song,
>   I'll sing Thy power to save.[4]

Where? In the company of "all the ransomed church of God" now "saved to sin no more."

And although our first priority must be to "tell the story" to those who have not yet heard, yet we sing

> I love to tell the story;
>   For those who know it best
> Seem hungering and thirsting
>   To hear it, like the rest.
> And when, in scenes of glory,
>   I sing the new, new song,
> 'Twill be the old, old story
>   That I have loved so long.[5]

Sometimes we sing good theology! But my point is that mission rests upon ultimate authority. The authority for the Christian mission is the revelation of God—Father, Son, and Holy Spirit—as a missionary God. Through the words of Scripture, through the testimony of the church, in the mystery of our inner selves, and in the midst of desperate human need, the living God confronts us as the one who has acted for our salvation in Jesus of Nazareth.

> I am sure we need constantly to remind ourselves that the imperative
> of the Church's mission to the world today rests solidly upon the

indicative of the mighty acts in the Incarnation, the Cross and the Resurrection, and that the dynamic for our unaccomplished task is the accomplished deed of God.[6]

Do we also need to remind ourselves that the revelation of God which validates our mission is not the authority of self-evident or scientific fact which must be accepted and cannot be denied? Our communication of the gospel by word, deed, and very life is a testimony of our faith in the living God who has come to us in Jesus Christ. Our witness is a confession of faith which cannot run roughshod over the beliefs of other persons and impose itself upon them. We do not have the right to make Christians out of people whether they want to be Christians or not. The authority under which we live and move and have our being is the authority which expects the response of faith, not the well-nigh inevitable assent demanded by self-evident fact. And faith must be free: our faith and everyone's faith, or it is not faith at all.

Why Are We Missionary?

To have a right to be missionary doesn't necessarily make one missionary. Authority for mission and motive for mission are not quite the same, though one moves easily into the other.

Nevertheless, motive is distinguishable from authority. Motive is not what validates mission or provides its foundation. Rather it is what impels the church or the individual Christian to be missionary, to seek to accomplish Christ's mission.

If you were to ask individual missionaries or earnest Christians who do not claim that title, what motivates them to participate in Christ's mission you might get about as many answers as the number of people you asked!

In a perceptive article, Creighton Lacy discussed several motives for mission expressed by different persons: to obey the Great Commission, to save one's own soul, to save the lost from hell, to transform cultures, to atone for exploitation, to render service, to protect the world from destructive forces, to prepare for the last judgment, to fulfill the very definition of the church, to express gratitude for the love of God made manifest in Jesus Christ. Lacy concluded that "there is no one Christian motivation for mission." The motivations "may be as varied as the functions or activities performed. They are

Christian to the extent that they find their imperative in the love of God as revealed in Jesus Christ."7

Undoubtedly, actual motives vary with individual Christians. Motive is much more subjective than authority, and human beings are very diverse. Many differing expressions of motive may indeed be valid, as Lacy indicates.

What I should like to suggest is a basic understanding of motive which can embrace individual variations on the same theme. I understand the basic motive of the Christian mission as grateful, loving response to the living God who has revealed himself to us graciously in Jesus Christ. We try to do his will and we seek his glory because we know him as alone worthy of our full devotion (Rev. 4:8-11; 5:9-14, etc.). We love him because he first loved us (1 John 4:7-12). We love the world because it is his creation. We forgive because he forgives (Eph. 4:32). We become ambassadors for Christ because God has reconciled us to himself in Christ and has given us the ministry of reconciliation (2 Cor. 5:18).

If the fundamental meaning of the gospel is grace, then is not the basic response gratitude?

So the Christian mission moves "forward through the ages" with joyous urgency impelled by gratitude.

The late E. Stanley Jones—noted missionary to India, world evangelist, and prolific author—carried youthful zest and prodigious energy into his old age. His autobiography, written in his eighties, he described as "my song of the pilgrimage I am making from what I was to what God is making of me."8 He tells of the physical and emotional illness which threatened to end his missionary career in its early beginnings and of the miraculous healing he experienced.9 Dr. Jones testified that God "sent me singing through the years."

Perhaps there is a parable here of the pilgrimage of the church. Often beset by "illnesses" and calamities, both self-induced and imposed from without, the church finds periodic healing and renewal. God's people are sent singing through the ages. "Bound by God's far purpose" in a joyous urgency, we move together toward "the shining goal."

"God's Far Purpose": What Is the Goal of Mission?

But what is "God's far purpose"? What is that "one far-off, divine event to which the whole creation moves?"[10] And how is the Christian mission related to it? What is the Christian mission pressing toward?

If, as we have claimed, the bold Christian mission proceeding through the ages and confronting all cultures requires an ultimate authority, then it must also have an ultimate goal.

One can conceive of many secondary goals for mission. Making disciples, for example, is certainly a legitimate objective. Jesus instructed us to "make disciples of all nations," did he not? But the question of ultimacy presses beyond this goal: Making disciples for what? To what end? The same is true of the planting of churches: a very worthy aim, but why plant churches? For what ultimate purpose? Or, some might suggest liberation as a goal, liberation from the bondage of sin, fear, oppression, etc. But liberation for what?

Let us remember that we are talking about a mission which is primarily God's work which he has called us to share. And what God is up to, according to the Bible, is the kingdom of God or the kingdom of heaven. The goal of mission, therefore, is the kingdom of God.

The Kingdom of God: God's New Order

Perhaps the term Kingdom does not communicate well in our day. In biblical times, kingdoms or monarchies were the usual political order. Now, however, monarchies are mostly out of favor as well as out-of-date. Hence the term *kingdom of God* is problematical for some.

I often use synonyms such as "God's new creation" or "God's new order" to convey something of the essential meaning without the negative connotations of "Kingdom." We are privileged to participate in a new order in which God is making all things new.

Now what is this kingdom of God, this new order? As God's kingdom it is transcendent and not subject to neat definitions, just as God cannot be defined! Jesus expressed its meaning in many parables and signs. I venture some positive statements about it, therefore, only very tentatively.

The kingdom of God is the expression of God's sovereign control over history. This purposive control is not yet fully evident. There is an old order of things in which the powers of evil are at work. God has placed all things under the gracious sovereignty of Christ (1 Cor. 15:27). But the process of overcoming all the enemies of Christ, the powers of the old order, will continue until the end, and "The last enemy to be defeated will be death" (1 Cor. 15:25-26, GNB).

So God's new order is both present and future. Jesus announced that "the kingdom of God is at hand" (Mark 1:15), or "the kingdom of God is in the midst of you" (Luke 17:21). But he also instructed his disciples to pray that the Kingdom might come (Matt. 6:10). At the appearing of the Son of man as King in judgment, the righteous will "inherit the kingdom" (Matt. 25:34). The Kingdom is here with us in history, but it transcends history as the perfect norm which judges everything human as incomplete and imperfect.

God's kingdom is the first priority of human beings. It is salvation for us and our world. We are to set our minds on "God's kingdom and his justice" (Matt. 6:33, NEB). We are to "Strive to enter by the narrow door" (Luke 13:24). This new order requires a radical turn-about and an unreserved commitment of faith: "No one who puts his hand to the plow and looks back is fit for the kingdom of God" (Luke 9:62). "Unless you turn round and become like children, you will never enter the kingdom of Heaven" (Matt. 18:3, NEB). Yet this new order is also God's gift of grace: "Fear not, little flock, for it is your Father's good pleasure to give you the kingdom" (Luke 12:32). The Kingdom is present in the fullness of its demand and promise but not in the shape of its final consummation.

According to the prophetic visions of Scripture, the kingdom of God in its completion is a transformed, redeemed universe at peace with itself and its Creator. It is truly a new order: "new heavens and a new earth, the home of justice" (2 Pet. 3:13, NEB; see also Isa. 2:2-4; 11:6-9; 65:17-25, etc.). At the center of the redeemed universe is the redeemed community, the city of God, the new Jerusalem (Heb. 11:10,16; 12:22-24; Rev. 21:1-4, 22-27; 22:1-5).

The Kingdom and the Mission

In these statements about the kingdom of God we can see hints of how it is the goal of the Christian mission, but let me be more explicit.

First of all, the gospel, which by means of the Christian mission is to be proclaimed to the whole creation, is the "good news of the kingdom of God." So mission testifies to the presence and the promise of the Kingdom. Jesus came preaching the good news that the Kingdom was finally at hand and calling upon all to repent and believe this good news (Mark 1:14-15). Later Jesus was to say, "This gospel of the kingdom will be preached throughout the whole world, as a testimony to all nations; and then the end will come" (Matt. 24:14).

So mission has to do with the good news of God's new order which has come into our world and our history in Jesus Christ. Mission is to continue until the end, testifying to this new creation until it has fully and finally come to pass. The goal of mission, then, is the end of history which the Bible understands as the full manifestation of the kingdom of God.

Second, the kingdom of God is the necessary goal of mission because nothing less is capable of embracing all worthy secondary objectives. Making disciples is an admirable objective, but disciples are to be made for the sake of the Kingdom and in the context of commitment to this new order. Planting churches is commendable, but churches exist to give witness to the Kingdom. Human liberation is an important missionary aim, but only God's new creation is the final liberation.

In fact, the kingdom of God gives breathtaking dimensions to the missionary task. The Kingdom is always expressive of God's priority concern with the poor and needy, the victims of injustice. Preaching good news to the poor, releasing the captives, bringing sight to the blind, liberating the oppressed, proclaiming the jubilee year of full freedom (Luke 4:18-19), all in radical commitment to the King and his Kingdom—what an awesome vision of the height and depth and breadth of mission!

But God's new order includes even more. It embraces the whole creation including the natural environment along with us humans. As we have noticed in chapter seven, the gospel is God's good news to the whole creation. He is not in the business of destroying his creation but transforming it into the new. And nature waits "with eager longing" and "groans with pain, like the pain of childbirth" for its full liberation along with the redeemed sons and daughters of God in the new creation (Rom. 8:18-23, GNB).

I believe it is time for the academic study of missions, which we call missiology, to address itself seriously to the question of missions and the nonhuman creation. The kingdom of God as the goal of mission gives ample room and impetus to such a new direction.

Third, the true universality of the mission of God which he calls us to share can be adequately understood and implemented only in terms of a universal goal: the new order which is the kingdom of God.

Appointment service for Southern Baptist Foreign Missionaries.

The gospel is addressed to all nations and to the whole creation. However, in the Bible "nations" probably does not mean what we usually mean by the term. We understand a nation primarily as a political entity, a nation-state. Although the term has various meanings in biblical usage,[11] as objects of God's redemptive mission, the "nations" seem to represent the human race in all its diversity and particularities, cultural, national, racial, linguistic, etc. Revelation mentions "an eternal message of Good News to announce to the peoples of the earth, to every race, tribe, language, and nation" (14:6, GNB). Perhaps this statement is an amplified description of what usually in the Scriptures is simply called "nation."

Until all these diverse groupings of humanity have brought their "glory and honor" into the eternal city of God, the mission is unfinished. In that city of the new creation, "the glory of God is its light" and "the glory and honor of the nations" is its tribute (Rev. 21:23-26). The glory of God is the manifestation of his mysterious and unique character which evokes awe, obeisance, and praise. The glory and honor of the nations must surely be the notable achievements and unique characteristics of the various peoples of the earth which under God's creative sovereignty permanently enrich the eternal city.

Just how the glory of God is to be brought into union with the glory of the nations in the new creation must remain a mystery to be revealed finally at the consummation of history. Mission at least catches glimpses of its meaning when we see the different expressions of Christian faith in various cultures and subcultures as we invite the "nations" to discipleship. And what a travesty it is if our missionary efforts help to destroy rather than preserve and transform the riches of diverse cultures!

Finally, a vital way of understanding the Christian mission is to see it as setting forth signs of the kingdom of God which is its final goal. Jesus the Messiah by his own works demonstrated that the promised new age had now come into our history. In his "inaugural sermon" at Nazareth he read from the prophecies of Isaiah describing the works of the messianic age and then announced, "Today this scripture has been fulfilled in your hearing" (Luke 4:16-21).

Similarly, when John the Baptist sent his disciples to ask Jesus whether he was the one "who is to come," Jesus told them to report to John what was being done, again citing prophecies of Isaiah: "The blind receive their sight, the lame walk, lepers are cleansed, and the deaf hear, the dead are raised up, the poor have good news preached to them" (Luke 7:22. See Matt. 11:5). That is, the works of the messianic kingdom were actually being done. Again, in the face of vicious criticism, Jesus reminded his accusers, "If it is by the Spirit of God that I cast out demons, then the kingdom of God has come upon you" (Matt. 12:28. See Luke 11:20).

The works of Jesus, then, were signs of the Kingdom, God's new order, breaking into our history and our world. What we do also must be signs of the Kingdom, for he tells us, "As the Father has sent me, even so I send you" (John 20:21). And he also says, "Truly, truly, I say to you, he who believes in me will also do the works that I do" (John 14:12).

Our mission is to serve the purposes of the Kingdom. Or, more specifically, it is service to the King who is the greatest Servant of all. The Kingdom itself turns out to be the heritage of those who have served the needy; serving the least of the brothers and sisters in need is to serve the King himself (Matt. 25:31 ff.).

We also know that when we understand ourselves and our service best, what we do in the name of the King/Servant is not nearly so much what we do as what he does in and through us. Both we and our service are actually the gifts of his grace: "Not I, but the grace of God which is with me" (1 Cor. 15:10).

The King of the new creation is at work in his world. He has come and initiated the new order by his incarnation, cross, and resurrection. In his risen life and presence in the Spirit he continues his work in his body, the church. Our mission is first of all his sovereign mission which he invites us to share. He is in our midst incognito and so is his kingly rule. Nevertheless we see its signs and we participate in setting them forth.

For about 250 years edict boards were erected in Japan prohibiting Christianity in the name and authority of the emperor. Any Christian or anyone harboring Christians was to be executed. These edict boards were finally removed in the 1870s.

By the Christian mission we are erecting in every diverse human group the edict boards of the Sovereign/Servant of the eternal Kingdom. These placards do not threaten life. Rather, they invite all to become heirs of eternal life and participants in the new order.

We are "bound by God's far purpose." Behind the veil of history, history with its complexities, contradictions and mysteries, the fabric of the new order is being woven. Hidden from us, the King weaves into it every loving act. It is not complete without our service. We are part of the offering of the glory and honor of the nations. Finishing the fabric of the Kingdom is the goal of our mission.

Who Are the Missionaries?

Who are the participants in the Christian mission? Thus far we have used the term *missionary* in the sense of some special calling while at the same time implying that all Christians are missionaries. It is important to look more closely at this question.

Missionary simply means "one who is sent." In normal usage, however, it connotes a bit more than that. It means "one who is commissioned and sent," or "one who is sent with an assignment."

Interestingly, in hardly any of the more familiar translations of the New Testament do you find the term *missionary*. Were there no missionaries in the early church? Of course there were! Then why don't we find the term in the New Testament? The answer is that although the word meaning missionary is found several times in the New Testament, it is a term used with more than one meaning. Therefore, translators usually transliterate it rather than translate it.

Apostles, The Twelve, and Others

The most natural term for missionary in Greek is *apostolos* transliterated into English as "apostle" and meaning literally "one sent forth" and hence "missionary" or "messenger." However, in the New Testament the term *apostle* not only has this ordinary meaning but also a more specialized one. In the Gospels it refers to the twelve Apostles, and in the early chapters of Acts it has this same usage except that a few others may share the role or status of the twelve, notably James, the brother of the Lord, and Paul. In this special sense, the apostles were those witnesses of the resurrection of Jesus who had been directly commissioned by the risen Lord to communicate the gospel. Thus understood, "apostle" referred to an office of special authority which by its nature could hardly continue beyond the first generation of Christians.

A tendency seems to have emerged during the New Testament period to reserve the title of apostle for this special meaning and to avoid using it for the more natural meaning of "missionary." For instance, the itinerant ministers mentioned in 3 John 5-8 quite appropriately might have been called missionaries. "It was on Christ's work that they went out; and they would accept nothing from pagans," says this letter. "We are bound to support such men, and so play our part in spreading the truth" (NEB). This refusal to expect support from the "pagans" is a principle followed by Paul in his missionary work (1 Cor. 9:3 ff.). But the itinerants mentioned in 3 John are not called missionaries but simply "brethren" and "strangers." By contrast, in the *Teaching of the Twelve*, a Christian writing of the first half of the second century, similar itinerants are aptly called "apostles [missionaries] and prophets."[12]

Before long this tendency to limit the term *apostle* to the twelve (and Paul and James) became universal.[13] In the early fourth century, for example, Eusebius, the famous church historian, refers to individuals who obviously did the work of missionaries as "evangelists"[14] He included among these "evangelists" Pantaenus, who was reputed to have gone to India.

So from New Testament times on there were missionaries, whether they rated the title *apostolos* or not. That is, there were those who understood themselves to have been specially called to communicate the gospel to those who had not yet believed or to strengthen the faith and witness of those who had recently believed. Some are mentioned in Acts: Philip, Peter, Barnabas, Saul (Paul), John Mark, Silas, Timothy, etc. And here and there in Acts and the Epistles the term *apostle* is used with the meaning of missionary.[15]

Missionaries, in this sense of a special calling, were persons impelled by the Holy Spirit to communicate the meaning of Jesus Christ on a frontier where the gospel met the world. Ordinarily, they were recognized and supported by churches. After New Testament times, as churchly organization developed, they were sent by ecclesiastical authorities, monasteries, etc. Hence the pattern today of sending missionaries by denominational, interdenominational, or nondenominational boards and societies.

Both Men and Women

Until the development of Protestantism, missions were almost entirely a masculine undertaking. An exception was the utilization of nuns in the work of the great missionary Boniface in European missions in the eighth century. In modern missions, however, both Catholic and Protestant, women have played a significant part.

From the beginning of American Protestant missions, missionary wives shared with their husbands the sacrifices and rigors of missionary life both in foreign missions and in home missions, especially Indian missions. Yet for a long time they, along with unordained men, were frequently designated "assistant missionaries" and had no vote in the mission organizations. Single women, far more than missionary wives, had to win a place in missions which they did heroically. By the 1920s, unmarried women had come to comprise the largest category of American missionaries.[16]

Single women, as well as missionary wives, not only pioneered in work with women and children but also engaged in all other kinds of missionary ministries except functions for which ordination was required. Of course, in some denominations eventually ordination became possible for women.

Large numbers of these women missionaries were sent by the many women's societies which had developed in the nineteenth century. Gradually these women's agencies were merged with the general mission boards. Sad to say, though women missionaries outnumbered men, they usually had no more than token representation in missionary administration.

In more recent years, at least two important changes occurred. One was a drastic decline in the percentage of single women in the total number of American Protestant missionaries. It appears that the reasons are to be found in certain social changes in American life: the multiplication of vocational opportunities for women—in social work, for example—the younger age of marriage, etc.[17] A second change was that the role of homemaker for the missionary wife has had greatly increased emphasis, thus somewhat excluding missionary wives from ministries outside the home.[18]

With the strong movement for the equality of the sexes, the situation is again being altered, not only among career missionaries but also among all Christians. The roles of both sexes have been influenced and broadened. For example, as more women seek vocational fulfillment outside the home—though not necessarily to the exclusion of the role of wife and mother—men are assuming a larger share in the roles of parent and homemaker. To be sure, tension continues between the legitimate concerns for family and for ministry outside the home, especially during the child-rearing years. Nevertheless, there is increased hope that women along with men may be able to participate fully in the ministries for which the Holy Spirit equips them and to which he calls them and also to share equitably in the administration of missions.[19]

Marks of the Missionary

From this understanding of who the missionary is, it may be possible to suggest some of the essential marks of the missionary. First, there is the *sense of call,* the inner impulse to find one's place on the frontier where one's testimony to the gospel is needed, an impulse from the Spirit of Christ within.

Secondly, the missionary ministers *on a frontier* where the name and spirit of Christ need to be communicated in word, deed, and life. The missionary establishes the Christian presence on the frontier and there gives expression to the redeeming gospel.

Third, the missionary brings to the frontier *spiritual gifts* to exercise in the name of Christ. Consider the example of Paul. Already in his missionary ministry in the young church in Antioch no doubt Paul had exemplified many of the spiritual gifts *(charismata)* which he later discussed in his Corinthian correspondence: gifts of apostleship, prophecy, teaching, healing, helping, administration, etc. Or, to put it more mundanely, already he was theologian, apologist, scholar, administrator, teacher, pastor, evangelist, and encourager. All of these gifts the Spirit of Jesus deployed in the person of Paul on the frontier in Antioch, then on the farther frontiers of Asia Minor and Europe.

Fourth, the missionary vocation is marked by a *gift for crossing frontiers,* a holy restlessness, a centrifugal thrust, an apostolic urge to submerge one's life in a situation different from one's own. As Paul expressed it, "I have become all things to all men, that I might by all means save some" (1 Cor. 9:22). Or again, "It is my ambition to bring the Gospel to places where the very name of Christ has not been heard" (Rom. 15:20, NEB).

Finally, the missionary is a *sign of the church's frontier existence.* While the missionary represents the church on a frontier, in a more fundamental sense he or she reminds the church that its whole life in all its members is to be lived on the cutting and growing edges of the world's life. The special calling of the missionary to minister on an obvious frontier is a sign that the church everywhere lives a frontier existence.

The Whole Church and All Christians

Far from signaling to the church that it can do its missionary work by proxy, the special calling of the missionary is a beacon pointing the whole church to its universal missionary task. It is a sign that in the profoundest sense all Christians are missionaries because all are called to share Christ's redemptive mission in a not yet redeemed world. All are called to represent Christ, to be Christs to their neighbors, as Martin Luther put it.[20] All are called to find those places where the gospel must be shared, where the love of God and neighbor and the thirst for justice which Jesus embodied may be lived out in a sinful and often cruel world.

In this deeper sense, one can hardly cross a street or a threshold without overstepping a frontier boundary where faith meets unbelief, where love confronts injustice, where compassion is face-to-face with tragic human need. So the frontiersmanship of the missionary calls the whole church to the awareness of its missionary existence.

I have heard that the noted Indian churchman V. S. Azariah, Anglican Bishop of Dornakal, had each convert when being baptized to repeat the words of the apostle Paul, "Woe is me if I preach not the gospel!" Of course, what was meant was not preaching from some church pulpit but communicating the good news of Christ by one's life daily and by as many ways as there are individual Christians. In this fundamental sense we are all evangelists, we are all ministers, we are all missionaries. James S. Stewart said it well:

> The concern for world evangelization is not something tacked on to a man's personal Christianity, which he may take or leave as he chooses: it is rooted indefeasibly in the character of the God who has come to us in Jesus. Thus it can never be the province of a few enthusiasts, a sideline or specialty of those who happen to have a bent for it. It is the distinctive mark of being a Christian. To accept Christ is to enlist under a missionary banner. It is quite impossible to be (in the Pauline phrase) 'in Christ' and not participate in Christ's mission in the world. In fact, here is the surest test whether we have truly grasped what Christ was doing by his life and death and resurrection, or whether we have failed even to begin to understand the Gospel that He brought.[21]

So the church wherever it exists is to be the people of God on mission. The church is chosen and called, as God's priestly people who have received his mercy, to "declare the wonderful deeds of him who called you out of darkness into his marvelous light" (1 Pet. 2:9-10).

> We must say bluntly that when the Church ceases to be a mission, then she ceases to have any right to the titles by which she is adorned in the New Testament. Apart from actual engagement in the task of being Christ's ambassador to the world, the name "priests and kings unto God" is but a usurped title.[22]

The local congregation is of strategic importance. In at least four modes of its life it should be involved in mission. First, the ethical life of the members should be such as to support and not contradict the truth of the gospel as everywhere communicated. Attitudes and actions which have to do with justice, personhood, and human rights should derive from the revelation of God in Jesus Christ.

Second, Christians should interpret their secular employments as opportunities for Christian witness and the fulfillment of Christian vocation. Wherever its members are scattered on Monday morning, there the church should be at work fulfilling its mission.

Third, the congregation should be involved in "mission action" in its own community. The normal places of secular employment in which the members of the church are engaged are very significant, but there may be large areas of tragic need quite beyond them. Places of special need should be identified by means of community surveys so that the church's ministries may reach them in the name of Christ.

Finally, the local church should support relevant programs of missions, regional, national and international, beyond its own locality. This support should include informed interest, intelligent prayer, and sacrificial giving of funds as well as a willingness on the part of members to go on mission wherever the Lord may direct.

In a world threatened by forces which would annihilate life or make it hardly worth living for many, we are called to communicate the good news of God's new order in Jesus Christ—with joyous urgency.

> Bound by God's far purpose
> In one living whole,
> Move we on together
> To the shining goal.[23]

Notes

1. From the hymn "Forward through the Ages" by Frederick Hosmer. Copyright, Beacon Press.

2. See David J. Bosch, *Witness to the World* (Atlanta: John Knox Press, 1980), p. 81.

3. Hymn, "Break Thou the Bread of Life," by Mary A. Lathbury, *Baptist Hymnal* (Nashville: Convention Press, 1975), p. 138.

4. Hymn, "There is a Fountain," by William Cowper, *The Service Hymnal* (Chicago: Hope Publishing Company, 1935), p. 145.

5. Hymn, "I Love to Tell the Story," by Katherine Hankey, *Baptist Hymnal* (Nashville: Convention Press, 1975), p. 461.

6. James S. Stewart, *Thine Is the Kingdom* (New York: Charles Scribner's Sons, 1956), p. 7.

7. Creighton Lacy, "Motivation for Mission," *The Outlook* (Wake Forest: Southeastern Baptist Theological Seminary), 15, No. 6 (July-Aug. 1965), pp. 18-35.

8. E. Stanley Jones, *A Song of Ascents, A Spiritual Autobiography* (Nashville: Abingdon Press, 1968), p. 17.

9. Ibid., chapter 6.

10. Alfred Lord Tennyson, *In Memoriam,* edited by William J. Rolfe (New York: Houghton, Mifflin and Company, 1895) p. 163.

11. See "Nations," *Interpreter's Dictionary of the Bible,* 4 (New York: Abingdon Press, 1962), pp. 515,523.

12. *Ante-Nicene Fathers,* VII (Grand Rapids: Eerdmans Publishing Company, 1951), pp. 380-381.

13. The (third century?) *Recognitions of Clement* even represents the twelve apostles as cautioning that no apostle besides them is to be looked for. ibid., VIII, p. 142.

14. *Nicene and Post-Nicene Fathers,* I (Grand Rapids: Eerdmans Publishing Company, 1952), p. 169. See also p. 225.

15. *Apostolos* means "missionary" in Acts 14:4,14 and in Romans 16:7. In Hebrews 3:1 the term is used of Jesus, possibly with the meaning of "missionary"; possibly also it means "missionary" with reference to various persons in Romans 11:13, 1 Corinthians 15:7, Revelation 2:2 and so forth. In 2 Corinthians 8:23 and Philippians 2:25 it merely means "messenger."

16. R. Pierce Beaver, *American Protestant Women in World Mission* (Grand Rapids: Eerdmans Publishing Company, 1980), especially chapters 2 and 3.

17. See ibid., pp. 199-200.

18. R. Pierce Beaver, *The Missionary Between the Times,* (Garden City, N. Y.: Doubleday and Company, 1968), pp. 76-79.

19. See Joyce M. Bowers, "Roles of Married Women Missionaries: A Case Study," *International Bulletin of Missionary Research,* 8, No. 1 (Jan. 1984), pp. 4-7.

20. *Works of Martin Luther,* 2 (Philadelphia: Muhlenberg Press, 1943), pp. 337-339.

21. Stewart, *Thine Is the Kingdom,* pp. 14-15.

22. Lesslie Newbigin, *The Household* of God (New York: Friendship Press, 1954), pp 163-164.

23. Frederick L. Hosmer, "Forward Through the Ages," *Baptist Hymnal* (Nashville: Convention Press, 1975), p. 146.

Index

Abraham 41
Advance programs 80, 83
affluence, affluent 97, 98, 104
African Independent churches 27, 126
American (Northern) Baptists 9,13, 15,75,78,86
American Council of Churches 126
American Friends Service Committee 117
American Muslim Mission 69
Anabaptists 50,51
Anderson, Rufus 53
Andrews, C. F. 129
apostles, apostolos 50,135,145-146,151
Associated Missions of the International Council of Churches (TAM-ICCC) 33,40
atomic bomb 61-63
attitudes, non imperialistic 102-105
Augustinians 48
Azariah, V. S. 149

Baha'i, Baha'is 68,69, 118
Baha'u'llah 69
Baptist, Baptists 9,10,51-52,74-76,91,101
Baptist Missionary Society (British) 51-52
Baptist Triennial Convention 78
Baptist World Alliance 87,117
Barnabas 146
Bible translation 27
Biblical authority 110,135
Biblical revelation 83,135
Bold Mission Thrust 24,80-81,89
Boniface (Yynfrith) 46,146
Braaten, Carl 109,112
Brainerd, David 51
Buddhism, Buddhists 19,69, 70,94,128,131
Buhlmann, Walbert 38,39

Carey, William 51-52,55,56,123,132
Carr, Canon Burgess 101,111
Cauthen, Baker James 82,83
Centenary program, 78

Charlemagne 46-47
Christian, Christians 9,15,25-30,35,36, 43,44,45,46,113,117,123,127,129, 130,133,134,135,136,137,138, 149-150
Christian approach to persons of other religions 127-132
"Christian" empire 45
Christian unity and cooperation 123-127
Christianity, world status of 25-30
church development 77,88,89
church growth 27,29,85,89-90
Church of World Messianity 71
Church of South India 124
church unions 124,126
Church World Service 117
Consultation on Church Union (now Church of Christ Uniting (COCU) 88
colonialism 53-54,58-61,68,93-96,100, 109
comity 126
communication, communications revolution 64-65
Communism, Communist 27,29,66-67, 93,120
Confucianism 69,70-71,73
conservative evangelical missionary agencies 31-33
Constantine 45
Cooperative Program, 81
Cornelius 43
Costas, Orlando 95-96,111,112
councils of churches 124,126
creation, the whole creation 47,121-123
Crusades, Crusaders, Crusader's Sword 41,47,48
cults 69

denominations, denominational divisions 12,126
Divine Light Mission 70
Dominicans 47,48
Division of Overseas Ministries, National Council of Churches of

153